Work Play Love

A Visual Guide to Calling,
Career & the Mission of God

Mark R. Shaw

IVP Books

An imprint of InterVarsity Press
Downers Grove, Illinois

InterVarsity Press
P.O. Box 1400, Downers Grove, IL 60515-1426
ivpress.com
email@ivpress.com

InterVarsity Press® is the book-publishing division of InterVarsity Christian Fellowship/USA®, a movement of students and faculty active on campus at hundreds of universities, colleges and schools of nursing in the United States of America, and a member movement of the International Fellowship of Evangelical Students. For information about local and regional activities, visit intervarsity.org.

All Scripture quotations, unless otherwise indicated, are taken from THE HOLY BIBLE, NEW INTERNATIONAL VERSION®, NIV® *Copyright © 1973, 1978, 1984, 2011 by Biblica, Inc.™ Used by permission. All rights reserved worldwide.*

While any stories in this book are true, some names and identifying information may have been changed to protect the privacy of individuals.

Cover design: Cindy Kiple
Interior design: Beth McGill
Images: Yellow paper © Michael Henderson/iStockphoto
        Bows and arrows: © LokFung/iStockphoto
Line illustrations: Mark R. Shaw

ISBN 978-0-8308-3673-4 (print)
ISBN 978-0-8308-9664-6 (digital)

Printed in the United States of America ∞

Library of Congress Cataloging-in-Publication Data

Shaw, Mark, 1949-
  Work, play, love : a visual guide to calling, career, and the mission of God / Mark R. Shaw.
    pages cm
  Includes bibliographical references.
  ISBN 978-0-8308-3673-4 (pbk. : alk. paper)
  1. Christian life. 2. Self-actualization (Psychology)—Religious aspects—Christianity. 3.
Vocation—Christianity. I. Title.
  BV4501.3.S53133 2014
  248.4—dc23

                    2014023037

P	26	25	24	23	22	21	20	19	18	17	16	15	14	13	12	11	10	9	8	7	6	5	4	3	2	1
Y	36	35	34	33	32	31	30	29	28	27	26	25	24	23	22	21	20	19	18	17	16	15	14			

To Graham, Connor, Elliot and William,

masters of play and wisdom workers

for the next generation

Contents

Acknowledgments

Many people were involved in the making of this little book. My thanks to Andy Le Peau and Al Hsu of InterVarsity Press for seeing the potential of this project and making it stronger in many ways. Thanks to my agent, Pieter Kwant, for believing. Hannah Teague, one of my favorite millennials, read an early version of the manuscript and offered valuable suggestions. Students in my "Foundations" class at Africa International University in Nairobi, Kenya, will recognize many of the ideas found herein. The original idea for the course (and the seed of the book) was due to conversations with two close friends, Dr. George Renner and the late Dr. Douglas Carew, who is sorely missed. Reverend Tom Kenney of Peninsula Community Chapel listened patiently to many of the early ideas of this book as we walked the Nolan Trail in Newport News, Virginia. He and his wife, Mabel, provided a quiet sanctuary for the completion of this book in their lovely home in Yorktown. My thanks also to their daughter, Caroline, who read a very early version of chapters one and two. To my prayer partners, Rev. Fred Nyabera and Professor Samuel Ngewa, whose encouragement and intercession over many years cannot go unacknowledged. Thanks also goes to my mother, Ellen Shaw, for loving books and art so much, and to my late father, Reverend Paul M. Shaw, for loving the Bible. My son, Jonathan, and his wife, Kate, and my daughter, Anne, and her husband, Michael, have helped me fall in love with millennials. My four grandsons, to whom this book is dedicated, have taught me as much about play as all the books I have read. Lois, my wife of forty-three years, is, in so many ways, a true Lady Wisdom in my life. And to my Father Almighty, Lord of the new creation, playful praise now and forever more.

Introduction

Just about everything I know about work I learned selling newspapers. My first job was delivering the *Boston Globe* to the good people of Middleborough, Massachusetts, a sleepy New England village forty miles south of Boston and sixteen miles from historic Plymouth. I was fourteen. Five days a week I'd race my metallic blue Schwinn bicycle to Farrar's Corner Store at 444 Center Street, a fixture in town since 1898. Mr. Farrar, grandson of the founder, was my first boss. He was a giant of a man, kind but firm. He'd have all my papers ready for delivery when I arrived. All I had to do was pick them up, load them into the basket on my bike and then make my rounds. Christmas time was always the best because of the tips. Rainy days were the worst, not only because of the misery of riding in the rain but also because of the extra work of stuffing the *Globe* into plastic bags. Payday was great too.

Even as a fourteen-year-old paperboy I quickly learned that life was more than work. I needed to learn how to juggle other parts of life besides my paper

> Truly I tell you, anyone who will not receive the kingdom of God like a little child will never enter it.
> **LUKE 18:17**

> My lifetime ambition has been to combine the utmost seriousness of question with the utmost lightness of form.
> **MILAN KUNDERA**

route. There was play, for example. I loved rooting for the Red Sox and the Celtics. I loved playing sandlot baseball, football, basketball and golf. Whenever I wasn't in school or delivering papers, I was swinging a club, working on my curve or dodging tackles. Finding time for both work and play was a challenge.

And then there was love. I was smitten by Evie Frankl, the little Jewish girl down the street. Whatever time I had beyond school, work or play was spent driving by her house (on my bike) hoping to catch a fleeting glance or, best of all, hanging out with her on weekends.

But my love life wasn't just Evie. I had a father, a mother, two sisters and a cocker spaniel at home. I was also beginning to fall in love with God. I wasn't born into a church home. Sunday was just another day for most of my years growing up. But something real and magical was happening on the cosmic front, and it all had to be juggled with the competing worlds of work and play.

I guess I've never gotten over this question of how to juggle work, play and love, because here I am fifty years later, still driving down a new "Center Street" (Nairobi, Kenya), picking up my current "paper route" (teaching at a university in Africa) and trying to impress the girl in my life (Lois). And I am still trying to figure out where play fits in to the whole picture.

Work-life balance. It's a big question, one that is with us all our lives. And it is what this book is all about.

What This Book Is and Isn't About

This book is not about how to choose a career. There are great books and useful tests out there on that subject, and I invite the interested reader to consult them. This book is not about whether you should become a missionary or a pastor, although it may be of use to those who already know they have those particular callings.

This book is also not primarily a theology of work, although it deals with that issue. There are wonderful books about this by people I admire such as Tim Keller, Andy Crouch, Darrow Miller, Os Guinness and Paul Stevens, among others.

What then is it about? This book is about identifying that we all have not one calling but a whole cluster of callings. We are called to do certain kinds of work, be a certain kind of person and love in certain kinds of ways. I want to explore what that calling cluster is for most of us and how we can balance those callings in a way that leads to personal flourishing and relevance to the larger world. Another way of putting it is that I want to explore work-life balance, or how to get your work, play and love in sync. This book is written primarily to emerging adults, those between eighteen and thirty who sense that these three areas of life might be out of whack in some way or who are looking for ways to get more out of life in each of these areas.

For the millennial generation, the largest generation in American history, new models are needed that move beyond the old paradigms of work and life that grew out of the Industrial Revolution in the nineteenth century and the Information Revolution in the twentieth. Common expressions of these older paradigms include the workaholic model ("all work and no play") and the equally exhausting work hard–play hard model (in which one lurches from destructive and exhausting work patterns to destructive and exhausting play patterns). Emerging adults deserve better models than these. I do hope it also reaches some of my own generation who, like me, are still trying to figure out the balance even as retirement looms ahead. And if you are in between millennials and boomers, I believe there is much in this book for you as well.

The work-life balance model that I propose in this book is one that I call the "wisdom worker" model. This is a model rooted in the wisdom of the Bible, particularly in the book of Proverbs but promoted throughout the Bible from Genesis to Revelation.

The model goes something like this: wisdom work consists of bringing a new "spirit" of work into every area of life—work, normal play and love. This new spirit is revealed in Proverbs 8 and is elaborated on and unleashed throughout the great story arc of the Hebrew and Christian Scriptures.

This new spirit of work, wisdom work, has three defining delights. First is learning to delight in whatever I am doing at any moment. Second is learning how to delight in whomever I am doing all of this with and for. And finally, wisdom work is about delighting in all of the above because God is at work everywhere around me and in me, making all things new (the "wherever"). The wisdom worker is one who learns how to bring these three delights into each of the three spheres of life. When I fill work, play and love with these three delights, good things begin to happen. My life finds balance. My work, play and love thrive and flourish in new and exciting ways. And I find new levels of happiness.

What surprised me most when I discovered the wisdom worker model is the role of play in achieving this new balance and vitality. The book of Proverbs presents wisdom work as a special kind of play, what I will call primary play. It is a fun, refreshing and profound way of working, playing and loving. The basic equation I develop in the pages that follow is "wisdom work = primary play." When primary play fills our work, play and love, life is good, hearts are satisfied and we become relevant to the mission of God.

For those who may wonder whether my three-word title is playing off Elizabeth Gilbert's *Eat, Pray, Love* or Anne Lamott's *Help, Thanks, Wow*, my only comment is that the distant echo to those books is unintentional. The reason for the title *Work, Play, Love* is simply that this is what the book is about—on every page.

Why the Pictures?

One feature of this book that may seem strange, unnecessary or even annoying to some readers is the use of "back of the napkin"–type sketches throughout to illustrate the main ideas of each chapter.

There are a number of reasons why I use both words and pictures in this book. The first is demographics. The emerging generation in North America is one of the most visually oriented in history. They are open to new experiments in visual thinking. Some of the great books in the past that dealt with calling, career and work-life balance may not have the same appeal to this demographic as they had to boomers.

The second reason has to do with the limitation of verbal communication. Dan Roam, in his bestseller *Blah, Blah, Blah: What to Do When Words Don't Work*,[1] suggests that three common limits to business communication are "Blah," "Blah, Blah" and "Blah, Blah, Blah." "Blah" is communication that is thin on content, rehashing clichés and truisms. "Blah, Blah" is speech that hides its message in an avalanche of verbiage and jargon. "Blah, Blah, Blah" is the worst kind of communication, far more dangerous than either superficiality or obscurity. It is propaganda, communication that is intended to deceive, misinform and manipulate.

To overcome these three limits of verbal communication, Roam calls for "vivid" communication. For Roam, the communication equation we need in the modern world is "verbal plus visual plus interdependence = vivid." Simple drawings and diagrams integrated ("interdependence") with text that is clear and truthful can help overcome the "blahs" of modern communication. "Back of the napkin"–type art has the potential to cut through the fog and lies and produce heightened understanding.

The third reason for pictures is my goal as a writer. I chose this particular way of creating a book rather than a more conventional approach because of the ability of "lightness" to free a world heavy with oppressive power. The power of artistic lightness is a theme developed by Czech novelist Milan Kundera, who lived and worked under the heaviness of communism. His novels are about little people trapped in the power games of the totalitarian state. He wrote against the background of a cultural nihilism that regarded God, humanity, reason and morality as "weightless" concepts without meaning. Only political power was real. Kundera's characters fight back against Big Brother by using their "weightlessness" and "lightness" to undermine ideology and power. His most famous novel, *The Unbearable Lightness of Being* (1984), follows the story of two men, two women and a dog through the tragic events of the Prague spring of 1968 when a repressive Soviet regime crushed the new political and artistic expressions taking place.

In an interview in the *Paris Review*, Kundera spoke of how he developed an "artistic style," a way of writing, that did inform what his novel attempted to do in content.[2] He not only wrote about characters who lived lives of subversive "lightness" but also sought a style of writing that fit that message. Kundera suggested that his goal as a writer confronting the abuses of power was to combine *"the utmost seriousness of question with the utmost lightness of form."*[3] Kundera rejected the dichotomy that serious subjects could only be spoken of in serious ways and that light subjects could only be spoken of in frivolous ways. In the postmodern world the best way to subvert the pretensions of power is to mix and match form and content. The "trivial" is freed to serve the truth, and the truth is liberated from the hands of the powerful or learned to partner with the playful to accomplish a common purpose.

My goal in writing vividly is the same. I write about some of the most serious questions of life, questions of purpose, work, play, love and God. I take the Bible and theology seriously. But this book could be just another expression of the "will to power." Lightness of form (doodles) means, however, that I am not able to intimidate or coerce by scholarship or Scripture. The message's content is of first importance, but its lightness of form frees the reader to taste without being trapped. It is my feeble attempt at combining the "utmost seriousness of question with the utmost lightness of form."

The final reason for the pictures is theological. Jesus taught playfully. He taught in parables, simple word pictures that carried his teaching in a way that reached all kinds of people in many generations and cultures. His first miracle took place at a wedding when he turned water into wine. Jesus was not just being playful but also being proverbial—bringing the spirit of wisdom's play in Proverbs 8 into all that he was doing. Jesus embodied Proverbs 8 wisdom. But more was going on than just that. Jesus was also playful wisdom's creator.[4] Thus, how can I write a book about bringing a new kind of play into our work, play and love without doing it in a playful way warranted by both the command of wisdom in Proverbs and the example of Christ in the Gospels? I want to use words and pictures together to convey the message that playful work is the key to recovering the work-life balance. The medium, as they say, is the message.

And So . . .

I haven't been back to Middleborough in many years. My family moved away after I went off to college. Then there was graduate school, marriage, kids and a career in Africa. I don't know what happened to Farrar's Corner Store. I'm not sure the old sandlots where I played baseball are still there. I lost touch with Evie shortly after she went off to Brandeis University. I hope she is happy in her career and family, wherever she may be. But one thing remains unchanged: my search for great work, great play and great love at fourteen years of age was part of a timeless quest. Details may change, but the quest has stayed the same. I invite you, then, on a treasure hunt to seek the wisdom that will satisfy this longing for balance and wholeness. And don't be surprised if the greatest treasure you find is simply the recovery of something you lost.

chapter one

Lady Wisdom's Call to Play

Work. Play. Love. For most of us, this is what life is all about. People want great work, great play and great love. And they want these three key areas of life to be in harmony. They dream of an integrated life in which these different areas flourish together like a thriving tree.

Achieving this kind of integrated life, like many other things in life, is easier said than done. Sometimes these three areas of life don't play well together. We become expert jugglers trying to keep the three balls in the air and not let anything drop. Even more troublesome is that over time these three areas can clash with one another, reducing happiness and increasing frustration. Our work (when we can find it) consumes us. Our play exhausts us (draining our time, money and sleep), and our relationships suffer from all the energy expended in this work hard–play hard approach to life.

In a recent study of over five million workers

Emerging adults long for work-life balance

worldwide, researchers found that nearly one out of two were dissatisfied with their work-life balance.[1] Highest levels of satisfaction in work-life balance were registered in Latin America (70%) and the lowest levels in Europe (44%); North America was in the middle. These figures may well decrease as economic volatility and job insecurity drive up the amount of time we spend at work.

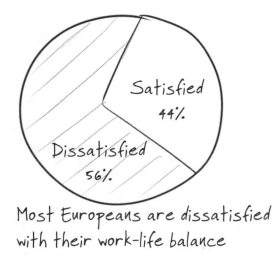

Most Europeans are dissatisfied with their work-life balance

For some employers, restoring work-life balance means little more than installing fitness machines in the employee lounge. Workers, however, want better relationships, more satisfying work and a host of other more intrinsic rewards for their labor, and research indicates that employees, rather than employers, may be the best source for restoring work-life balance in their lives. Jim Bird, president of worklifebalance.com, points to personal responsibility if one wants to find the "sweet spot" between satisfying work and a satisfying life. "The individual has to do it for themselves," says Bird. "Where companies can really make that happen is through training."[2]

Current Models of Work-Life Balance

One of the hurdles to taking control of our own work-life balance is the lack of good models. Consider the cases of Mike and Mia, both twentysomethings that care about these three areas of life but have trouble getting them to work in sync. Mike is a recent university graduate who found a job teaching high school in the inner city. Faith matters a lot to Mike. He also wants to make a difference in the inner city. But what does "making a difference" look like in a job? Mike's model of work is his father, a surgeon who seemed to live at the hospital. The first year teaching almost killed Mike. He poured himself into his work and his students. Eighty-hour weeks were the norm. In college, Mike used to love playing soccer and video games as ways to blow off steam. He would spend all night playing video football with his friends when the latest version of Madden NFL came out. He was also pretty involved in a campus ministry in his last year of graduate school. But those areas of life went out the window during that first year of teaching.

Work can get out of balance and threaten the other areas of life

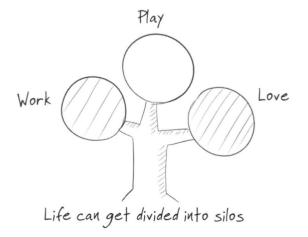

Life can get divided into silos

Then Mike met Erin, and everything changed. Erin challenged his all-work model of life. Erin had come from a home in which family and relationships were as important as work. Her mother had been an engineer in the auto industry but carefully balanced her role as an engineer with her other roles as mother, wife and Sunday school teacher. Erin's mom had also been an accomplished tennis player and played several times a week.

Mike appreciated this new model from Erin's family and tried it out in his own life. He made some real progress in bringing the balance back. He cut back his work to a more realistic fifty hours and began playing indoor soccer two nights a week. Weekends were for Erin and church. This new balance was a huge improvement, but Mike still struggled to keep all the balls in the air. There seemed to be very little flow between the three areas of his life. For Mike, work, play and love all seemed to be their own worlds with little energy being shared between them. He struggled to get his work done in time. He still felt guilty playing indoor soccer when he could have spent more time with Erin or grading papers. When he was with Erin on the weekends he found his mind drifting to work matters or wishing he had time to play a video game. There was balance in his life, but it was a sterile balance. He felt like his life was divided into separate silos.

Mia is a friend of Mike's who took a different approach to work-life balance. After graduation she went back home for a while but eventually found a job in marketing. She loved her work and her new colleagues for the most part. She also loved to party. She worked hard during the week but then went crazy on the weekends; this was the pattern that she had established at university. Mia justified her partying lifestyle as a way to deal with stress. Plus, she made a lot of friends. But there were consequences. Mia was so exhausted by her weekend activities that she was late for work a few days each week. Her productivity on Fridays was next to zero as she shifted focus to the weekend. One of her weekend revelers was recently fired for coming to work intoxicated. Mia didn't want to

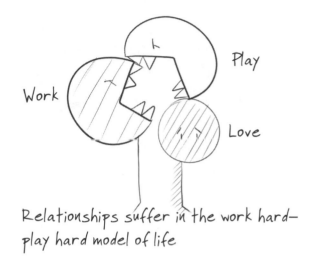

Relationships suffer in the work hard–play hard model of life

be next. It was a wake-up call. How far would she get in her career if she got fired from her first job for partying too hard? She had assumed that the work hard–play hard model of her high school and college friends was the normal way to live. Now she had second thoughts.

Looking for a Better Way

Each of these life-balance models has its advocates and exemplars. Millions of people live their whole lives according to the scripts written by the workaholic, the silo artist or the work hard–play hard acrobat. For many millennials, and even for their parents, these three scripts constitute their calling in life. But emerging adults deserve better options for work-life balance than these three traditional ones. Is there a better way?

I'd like to add a new model of work-life balance to the mix. I call it the "wisdom worker" model. The roots of this view are ancient. They are found in the book of Proverbs in the Hebrew Scriptures. Though Proverbs introduces the model, the rest of the Bible develops the wisdom worker model in profound and useful ways. What excites me about the model is that it works. I have found this model to be both life changing and highly productive. I also enjoy the way this model opens up the great story arc of the Bible, something called the mission of God, and shows us how to become relevant to this massive project that is both global and transformational. So I want to begin the search for answers to the work-life balance by taking a deeper look into the book of Proverbs.

Before I begin, however, I need to address why I use the Bible. For some readers, my starting point could be a problem. The Bible is a difficult book full

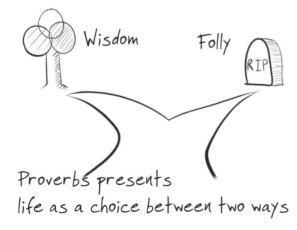

Proverbs presents
life as a choice between two ways

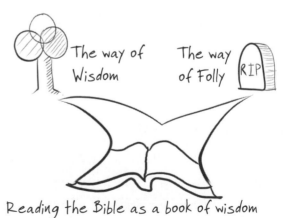

Reading the Bible as a book of wisdom

of controversial moral judgments and harsh doctrines. Why use this problematic source as a primary text for answering questions about work, play and love? I can appreciate this concern. My personal experience with the Bible, however, has been very different. I have, admittedly, found the Bible to be both difficult and controversial. But I have also found it to be so much more than that. The Bible has answered my big questions (the "Why am I here?" questions) as well as many of my smaller ones (for example, "How do I get my life in balance?"). No book I have ever encountered has changed my life and thinking about God, the world, humanity and the self as much as the Bible has. I have become convinced that God speaks through this book in a special and powerful way. But you don't need to share my personal convictions in order to go on this journey into the Bible with me. There is a good reason why even someone from another faith, or no faith, should take the Bible seriously—because it contains wisdom.

I want to read the Bible as a book of wisdom. Wisdom is decision making that leads to human flourishing. Folly is decision making that destroys life. Wisdom builds up. Folly tears down. Throughout history, in all societies, those two paths have been mapped out to help emerging generations choose life over death.

There are other ways to read the Bible. One can read it as literature out of curiosity. Or it might be read as doctrine that must be believed in order to belong to the church. One can use it liturgically to worship. It can also be read as a book of do's and don'ts that put us on guilt trips. Reading the Bible as wisdom uses the Bible slightly differently. In this approach, we seek to know how to make life flourish. In reading the Bible as a book of wisdom we may touch on all the other ways to read the Bible, but we never lose sight of the overarching question: what does the Bible say about how to make life work?

Proverbs and the Tree of Life

The book of Proverbs is difficult, if not impossible, to outline. However, even the casual reader can discern some central themes. Some of the main themes are how to live well, how to love well and how to work well. In other words, Proverbs addresses the same kinds of questions I am interested in. The great framework of the book is the two ways—the way of life and the way of death. Wisdom leads to life. "She is a tree of life to those who take hold of her; those who hold her fast will be blessed" (Proverbs 3:18). Folly, on the other hand, leads to death.

For centuries before the book of Proverbs was written, human civilizations were fascinated by this question of the two ways. The book of Proverbs makes use of the diverse and global wisdom of the time. Solomon, the author of much of Proverbs, presents the search for wisdom as the search for the appropriate norm or practical action for any situation in life. In that sense, wisdom is an inductive art, a quest for the secrets that will unlock great work, great engineering, great relationships or great wealth. For Solomon, however, wisdom has a single, *master norm* that makes possible practical and profitable use of all the "little" norms of life and work. Three times in the book he refers to it as "the fear of God," which should be taken to mean awesome regard. In Proverbs 3:5-6 he refers to this master norm in a slightly different way. Wisdom is trusting in "the LORD with all [our] heart" and not leaning on limited human understanding alone. Wisdom's master norm is to depend on God in every way, believing that he will "make [our] paths straight," that is, lead us to success. Solomon uses these first nine chapters as an extended prologue to the collection of work, play and love norms found in chapters 11 through 31. He takes the role of a father teaching his son how to live well, introducing the young prince to Lady Wisdom—not a real character but rather a personification of wisdom.

Wisdom for Solomon then is a double quest. First, wisdom is the search for the norms of success in everyday life. Second, wisdom is the exploration of the depths of the master norm of awe and trust in God declared in chapter 3. Chapters 11 through 31 focus on the search for the "little" norms.

Chapters 1 through 9, climaxing in chapter 8, are Solomon's exploration of the master norm of radical trust in God in all of life. Chapter 8 is the key. Tremper Longman, in his commentary on Proverbs, argues that chapter 8 is the climax of the entire book.[3] Old Testament scholar Samuel Terrien declares that Lady's Wisdom's poem in 8:22-31 "should be considered the pivot of scripture, the motif that, more than any other, leads from the Old Testament to the New."[4]

Chapter 8 opens with Lady Wisdom standing on a busy street in the city center, crying out to men passing by indifferent to her plea: "To you, O people, I call out; I raise my voice to all mankind" (v. 4). Wisdom stands on the street corner soliciting all people everywhere ("all mankind") to take her and her call

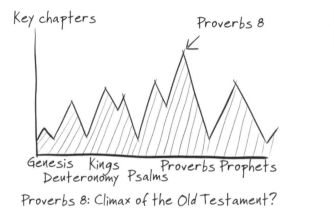

Proverbs 8: Climax of the Old Testament?

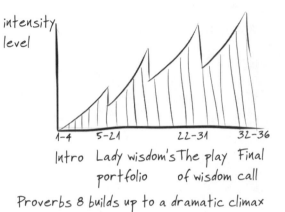

Proverbs 8 builds up to a dramatic climax

seriously. She comes across more like a shameless prostitute than Solomon's vaunted lady of prudence and honor. Why her rude behavior? She is not soliciting humanity in order to exploit but rather to point out the most exciting secret she has, the secret of secrets. She knows something everyone needs to know in order to live well. Her secret is the very secret of life. She has abandoned her dignity in a desperate attempt to help humanity find her treasure and live rather than miss it and die. When she feels she has the attention of the crowd she introduces herself, giving highlights of her résumé and all the reasons why someone should listen to her (vv. 5-21). The climax of the chapter is when Wisdom breaks into song (or at least a poem) in verses 22-31. It is here that she gives her pearl of wisdom—the secret of life, work and love. The chapter ends with Wisdom giving her final appeal and warning to the listener in verses 32-36.

I want to focus for a moment on verses 22 to 36. Scholars call this section "the Play of Wisdom." She sings excitedly about what she discovered about work,

Breaking down the song of wisdom and the secret of life in Proverbs 8:22-36

play and love. The song has three movements. The first, in verses 22-29, tells us what Wisdom saw. The second movement, verses 30-31, tells us what Wisdom did, and the final movement, verses 32-36, tells us what Wisdom wants of us.

What Wisdom Saw: From Nothingness to New Creation

Wisdom begins by telling us about her birth. She came into existence, she says, before anything else existed. When Wisdom opened her eyes at the dawn of time she saw, well, nothing at all. Wisdom begins her life and work staring into the void. She was created for a new world, for she alone has all the norms needed for that new world to grow and flourish. But she arrives before the new world is anywhere to be seen. She must have puzzled over the emptiness all around her, so overflowing is she with the laws of science and success dancing in her head.

GOD sovereignly made me—the first, the basic—
    before he did anything else.
I was brought into being a long time ago,
    well before Earth got its start.
I arrived on the scene before Ocean,
    yes, even before Springs and Rivers and Lakes.
Before Mountains were sculpted and Hills took shape,
    I was already there, newborn;
Long before GOD stretched out Earth's Horizons,
    and tended to the minute details of Soil and Weather,
And set Sky firmly in place,
    I was there.
When he mapped and gave borders to wild Ocean,
    built the vast vault of Heaven,
    and installed the fountains that fed Ocean,
When he drew a boundary for Sea,
    posted a sign that said NO TRESPASSING,
And then staked out Earth's Foundations,
    I was right there with him, making sure everything fit.

PROVERBS 8:22-29 *THE MESSAGE*

She does not puzzle long, however. As she stares into the void she feels the presence of another. She is not alone. She turns and sees where she is. She is in the arms of her Father. God stares into that void with her. He does more than stare, however. He acts. Out of nothing comes everything. By his mere word, her almighty Father makes earth and sky, sea and land, rivers and snowflakes. A billion stars blink at her where just a moment before there was only blackness. Wisdom's role is not primarily to do but to be, to see with eyes of awe and love the breathtaking work of her Father. She is there first and foremost as a much-loved child in the Father's arms, witnessing her parent's work.

Soon she will join him in the work. But for now, before she fills the world with the norms that lead to life, she discovers the norm of norms, life's great master norm—that we were made to love, trust and enjoy a God who alone makes all things out of nothing. Infant Wisdom is overcome with awe and excitement when ugliness is turned into beauty, chaos into order and silence

Wisdom is
born, v. 22

Wisdom
opens her
eyes, v. 23

There was
nothing there!

Wisdom awakens to nothingness

As wisdom stares into the void, God acts
and makes everything out of nothing

into the symphony of life. By her careful observation of her Father at work, she realizes the primary presupposition of all truth about life: without God, nothing. With God, everything. God does not need to create, nor does he need any help in creating. He does it all. There is no evil, no folly, no force that can resist him. He speaks and it is. God created Wisdom to be a witness to all humanity that an almighty Father is at work everywhere around us making all things new. God is the one who makes everyone and everything fully and finally alive. That is what she saw when she opened her eyes. God and God alone. A God from whom all blessings flow, from whom all reality flows. The source of all that exists, all that is beautiful, all that is life-giving and good.

What Wisdom Did: Playful Partnership

Wisdom is more than just a much-loved daughter of an almighty Father. She does more than just watch as her Father goes about his work of creation, spreading it over vast stretches of creation time. She is also a coworker. Wisdom not only watches but also works.

In Proverbs 8:30 Wisdom describes herself as a "craftsman at his side." There is nothing in this world that Wisdom does not know everything about. Pluck any leaf and ask what we can do with it, and she will list dozens of uses. Dig any

Then I was the craftsman at his side.
I was filled with delight day after day,
*   rejoicing always in his presence,*
rejoicing in his whole world
*   and delighting in mankind.*

PROVERBS 8:30-31 NIV **1984**

mineral from the ground and she will tell you thousands of technologies, hundreds of industrial applications and dozens of other uses. Visit any hospital and Wisdom can tell you not only the causes of all maladies but the details of every cure. Point to any person and ask how they can find happiness, and she will have the exact formula and roadmap for that person's maximum happiness and fulfillment. She is a master craftsman of created things. She is an artisan of life. Most of her knowledge is still buried away in nature, history or the human heart, waiting to be discovered. She knows everything about how life in this world works because she was a partner with God when he was making life, the world and everything.

As God's partner in creation, Lady Wisdom knows everything about life and how it works

Her insights, discoveries, applications, inventions and science are comprehensive in scope. She knows everything about everything.

Since Wisdom knows the secret of living successfully, we bring to her and to this stanza of her song our simple question: What is the best way for us to do life and work and play? She looks up at us from the text, winks and then invites us to watch how she works in these verses so that we can imitate her.

In verses 30-31 she gives her secret: "Work like I work. If you want to get around with God, humanity and the world then learn how to play. Play is the secret of life."

Wisdom declares that her craftsmanlike partnership in creation is all about play. Twice in two verses the writer uses a Hebrew word for play (*mishak*). She plays with the Father, delighting in being at his side. She plays with humanity, delighted with these crowning achievements of creation. She plays with the world, dancing and laughing at the panorama around her. Most English translations of these verses miss out on the significance of *mishak*. Yet so important is this play of Wisdom that commentator Tremper Longman made his own translation from the Hebrew in order to bring out the force of this idea: "I was beside him as a craftsman. I was *playing* daily, *laughing* before him all the time. *Laughing* with all the inhabitants of the earth and *playing* with all the human race."[5]

Longman is not alone in recognizing the importance of play in these verses. Another scholar, Hugh Matlack, captures the spirit of Lady Wisdom's playful work: "She plays before God all of the time, in the whole world and with all of humanity. Wisdom, like a child in the 'terrible two' stage, is into everything. She is everywhere, with everyone, all the time. Like a very young child, she sees and enjoys everything for the first time. She is the perfect witness to creation, itself brand new."[6]

All of this may sound strange to our ears. What kind of play is Wisdom engaged in? It is certainly not play as I know it. I know play as something confined to one part of life. For me, play is a way to blow off steam, get some exercise, have a laugh or kill time. Play is trivializing our life away. This special play,

Wisdom works by playing with
the Father in all of life

however, is one that fills all of work, all of life. It is a spirit or attitude that Wisdom brings with her into her partnership in creation as she and her almighty Father bring everything out of nothing and make all things new.

The term I will use in this book for the special play of wisdom is *primary play*—the first kind of play and the kind of play that must be first in all we do. What is primary play? Wisdom tells me at least three important things in these two verses about working in playful partnership with God. First, primary play is about seeing God as an almighty Father who is at work all around us making everything and everyone new. Unless I see God as one who eliminates fear and failure from the human story, I will not be able to play as Wisdom played. Those who work like Wisdom works must be as fearless as she is in a world made safe by her Creator.

Second, primary play is partnering with God in making all things new. "I was a craftsman at his side." Wisdom has every norm at her disposal. She has a comprehensive knowledge of science, technology, learning, life, success, prosperity and happiness. But this is not enough for her. Along with her "omni-competence" comes an "omni-playfulness." Everything she does is done in playful partnership with God.

Third, primary play is about bringing this playful seeing and partnering into whatever I do and into all my relationships. Wisdom playfully delights in whatever she is doing at her Father's side. She also delights in all humanity. Her play is not a substitute for being a craftsman. The hard work remains. Yet behind the search for and mastery of the "little" norms of work, play and love must be something more, a master norm of cosmic playfulness, laughter and celebration.

What does all this imply about our work-life balance? Primary play needs our attention. This is working as Wisdom works. And the work of wisdom is playing the game of life with three important rules.

First, becoming a wisdom worker means playfully delighting in whatever we do each day. I will call this first delight the *whatever*. Second, it means playfully delighting in whomever we do it all with and for. I will call this the *whomever*. Third, it means making my delight in my almighty Father, who is at work everywhere around me and in me making all things new, the delight that drives all other delights. I will call this the *wherever* (as in, God

3. Delight in God who is at work everywhere around her

1. Delight in whatever she does

2. Delight in whomever she does her work with and for

How wisdom works

3. Delight that God is at work everywhere

1. Delight in whatever one does

2. Delight in whomever one does it all with and for

How we should work

is at work everywhere around us and in us). As Lady Wisdom's song testifies, one can playfully do the whatever and the whomever only because of the wherever.

To work like Wisdom works means more than just "doing my duty" or "managing my responsibilities." When I bring this spirit of play into the realms of work, play and love, I will flourish in all areas, and balance will be restored. Wisdom sees something that I must see. She does work in a way that I must learn to do work. But that is not all. She also wants something that I need to want.

What Wisdom Wants: The Call to Primary Play

Wisdom is not finished in verse 31. In verse 32, she turns to us, her audience, and calls us to join her by becoming wisdom workers in our own day and time, people who bring the primary play of triple delight in God and his works into all that we do. Wisdom is back on the street issuing her final plea:

> *So, my dear friends, listen carefully;*
> *those who embrace these my ways are most blessed.*
> *Mark a life of discipline and live wisely;*
> *don't squander your precious life.*
> *Blessed the man, blessed the woman, who listens to me,*
> *awake and ready for me each morning,*
> *alert and responsive as I start my day's work.*
> *When you find me, you find life, real life,*
> *to say nothing of GOD's good pleasure.*
> *But if you wrong me, you damage your very soul;*
> *when you reject me, you're flirting with death.*
>
> **PROVERBS 8:32-36** *THE MESSAGE*

Wisdom's call is to "embrace my ways." Wisdom wants me to work like she works. She wants me to be a playful partner with God in his new creation project. For Wisdom this is not a call that you can fool around with. She is dead

The call of wisdom is to play or die

serious. To be a wisdom worker means bringing primary play into everything I do, including work, play and love. If I heed the call, I will live. If I ignore the call or treat it with contempt, I die. It's about as blunt as that. Wisdom work is not just one of many options. It is the only option. Play or die.

Questions About the Call of Wisdom

At this point there may be a few questions.

First, isn't calling a command from God to do something special like become an apostle, priest, pastor or missionary? Play seems like the opposite of a calling. Isn't play really just a break or diversion from our calling?

This question assumes that calling is a command from God that has to do with life purpose and little or nothing to do with play. Play, says the questioner, is a break or interruption from one's calling.

I agree that calling is from God. That at least was the answer given by Europeans in the Middle Ages. Calling was (largely) confined to becoming a priest or nun. We have come a long way from that view, however. During the Reformation of the sixteenth century, the idea of calling began to be applied to professions outside of religious ones. People began to see that a God-centered faith could turn farming, politics, raising kids, art or business into a spiritual vocation. In a secular age, however, this belief that any kind of work can be done for the glory of God has morphed into the idea that work itself is god—the fount of all of life's blessings.

There is good in the medieval idea that God calls people to preach his gospel and serve the spiritual needs of the world. There is good in the Reformation idea that any and all human pursuits can be done to the glory of God. There is good in the secular view that we should see our work as extremely important. But we need to take one more step in our evolving views on calling: we need the wisdom perspective of Proverbs 8 that our work should flow from the spontaneous delight of seeing God at work all around us, freeing us to playfully partner with him. This changes everything. Calling is no longer just a divine command to do a job. Calling is now a *divine invitation to playful partnership*. Every calling of God in the Bible, whether to life, work or love, is not primarily a command to perform but rather an invitation to play with him in the new creation that he is making. Everyday play may be a break from calling, but primary play is at the heart of every calling.

We need to change our assumptions about play. When many of us think of play we think of a little kid digging in the sandbox. But play is something that covers a wide range of adult activity, from the skillful guitarist to the professional athlete. What ties these activities and ages together is the playful attitude that leads to high performance. When Lionel Messi, one of the world's great soccer players, is on the field and his team is behind, he doesn't freak out or overthink. He forgets about the crowd, the clock and the score and enters a state of relaxed intensity that athletes call the "zone." In that zone they operate out of simple and pure delight. They love what they are doing. They delight in whomever they are doing it with and for. And they feel totally secure and safe in their surroundings, enabling them to focus on the task at hand and do their best. The call of wisdom is the call to live in the zone of relaxed intensity, the zone of kingdom play. Wisdom gives us the means to get in that zone (delighting in the whatever, the whomever and the wherever).

A second question that may arise concerns the "call to play." Am I making too much out of Proverbs 8? After all, the Bible contains multiple divine calls from Genesis to Revelation. We are called to work (Genesis 1), to holiness (Exodus 20), to worship (Isaiah 6 and the Psalms), to be born again (John 3), to disciple the nations (Matthew 28) and to serve the Lord in everything we do

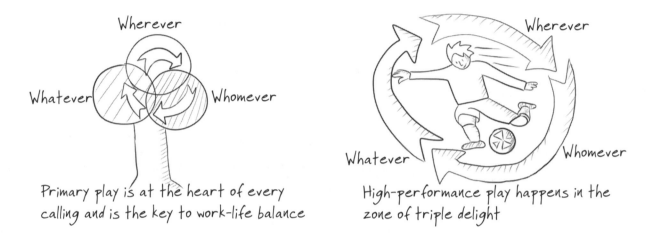

Primary play is at the heart of every calling and is the key to work-life balance

High-performance play happens in the zone of triple delight

(Colossians 3). Why pluck one strange and lonely calling out of the pile and claim it has some kind of priority? Good question. Let me give at least three reasons for the priority of wisdom's call to primary play.

First, it is the first call in history. The call to play with God in his new creation comes from before time began. It precedes even the call to work in Genesis 1. Second, the text itself claims it is the most important call of the Bible. Wisdom throws off most of her dignity in chapter 8, so desperate is she to get humanity to listen to this call. Few calls in the Old Testament contain such drama. This call, says Proverbs 8:4, is for all humanity. Not just some people but all people. Wisdom claims, at the end of chapter 8, that hearing and obeying her call is a matter of life and death. She has claimed earlier in Proverbs that the person who finds wisdom finds life. Any attempt to relativize this word of wisdom would contradict the clear message of not only this text but the rest of Bible, which consistently confirms the centrality of wisdom. Finally, this call to play is found throughout the Bible. When Colossians 1 proclaims Jesus as the fullness of all wisdom and knowledge who partnered with his almighty Father in creating all things, it is referencing Proverbs 8 (see Colossians 1:16-17 and also 2:3). When the Epistle of James calls the new churches of the Jesus movement to wisdom living, it is referencing Proverbs 8 (James 1:5; 3:15). When John in Revelation repeatedly praises wisdom and calls for wisdom in order to understand the new creation that is unfolding before his eyes, he is referencing Proverbs 8. In fact, so central is the wisdom theme in Scripture that faithful students of the Bible must see Proverbs 8 as a key hermeneutic that unlocks the Bible's main message (Revelation 5:12). So, no, the call to play is not just a minor note in the biblical symphony of calling. It is the piano.

Question three raises the issue of relevance. Why does Wisdom call me to work like this when the very circumstances she describes in chapter 8 (partnering with God in creation) no longer apply? Creation is over. How can her way of work be a model when the context is so different? The drama of Proverbs 8 is all about God creating the world. Wisdom was by his side in creating everything. He was the almighty Father who did everything with his much-loved child, not because he couldn't do it himself but out of love and play. But we are no longer at that point of history. The task of creation is long finished, and we now live in an aging universe in which, to quote the cynic of the book of Ecclesiastes, "there is nothing new under the sun" (Ecclesiastes 1:9). Furthermore we live in a world so broken by sin and evil that little of that good creation can even be seen anymore. The wisdom worker model simply isn't relevant for the current state of affairs, however useful it may have been in the world before time. So says the questioner.

My response is simple. The wisdom worker model is the most relevant model for our time. The great fact of our history and of all history is that God is at work, once again making all things new. This is the message of biblical hope. This message of an almighty Father at work to purge the "void" from his creation once and for all is the big news of the Bible. This "new creation" project is called the mission of God. The entire message of authentic Christian faith is that through Jesus Christ this broken world will be completely, comprehensively and conclusively healed. I, like Lady Wisdom, am born into the middle of this project. I see some beauty around me. I also see a lot of ugly. The new creation is not complete. My Father, just as he did with Wisdom, calls me to join him in his work by taking the work style of Wisdom as my model. Because he is now at work making all things new and because he cannot fail, I can work for his new creation without fear or futility. I stand in exactly the same place Wisdom once stood. I need her model of playful partnership with an almighty Father in order to be relevant to the mission of God in my time.

Question four brings us back to the main question of the book—work-life balance. How does all this talk of wisdom work and the call to play apply to my work-life balance? How does this wisdom worker model help? How does it overcome some of the deficiencies in the models presented at the beginning of the chapter (work hard–play hard, work is all or the silo model)? Is this call of

Lady Wisdom to play for the kingdom being pulled out of context from the rest of the Proverbs?

Lady Wisdom's call is very much in context. The whole book of Proverbs is about avoiding the work hard–play hard dichotomy of folly, the destructive play that leads to death. It is also suspicious of the "work is all" model of life balance. It looks with suspicion at the silo model that tries to keep all the areas of life separate but equal. Wisdom rejects these models of work life balance and instead points to the "playful partnership" model. That is to say, in all our work in the world, and all our rest, we should practice the "play of wisdom" by delighting in whatever we do, delighting in whomever we do it all with and for, and doing it all in the arms of an almighty Father, working everywhere to make all things new. When wisdom reaches that place of high-performance play and works from that center of pleasure and delight, it leads to life and prosperity. It avoids boring work and destructive play. It transforms everything.

How does it help in one's job or career? I might have a great boss, great co-workers, great space, great work and great pay. But this is not everyone's experience. Many emerging adults have trouble finding the type of work they want to do or the kind of work environment they want. This can be a rude awakening. But the wisdom worker, equipped with primary play, has a powerful tool in her hands. She can actually transform her workplace or her kind of work by the power of primary play. She doesn't have to wait for that great boss or that perfect job to come along. She practices the triple delight of Proverbs 8 (the whatever, the whomever and the wherever). She brings her capacity for delight with her.

Wisdom workers in the twenty-first century will be those who know how to bring the technique of playful delight into their work. Our work may be a "void," an environment that does not foster human flourishing. Yet by answering the call of wisdom we will learn how to playfully partner with God in whatever we do and wherever we work. The play of wisdom empowers us to enter the "void" and engage our work and our workmates with delight. Only wisdom work can produce this new power to shape a new environment. It is practical and it is powerful.

People want great work, great play and great love. They want work-life balance. But life seems to frustrate that dream. I am convinced that emerging adults will not get what they want and need from existing models of work-life balance. Improved models are needed, and Proverbs 8 and the wisdom worker/playful partner model is the improvement that the rising generation is looking for. The most surprising feature of this model is the role of play. Primary play, according to Lady Wisdom, is the key to the integration and expansion of our work, play and love. This is the key to the life I and many others want. But how do we move from ancient texts to modern contexts? How do we practice what Lady Wisdom preaches? This is the important question we now turn to.

Thinking It Through

1. As you think of the three key areas of life—work, play and love—how in balance are these areas in your life right now? Draw a picture making the circles bigger or smaller depending on which areas seem to be more dominant or more neglected.

2. To what degree are these three areas kept in silos? Do you feel that your work is separated from play and your play from work? Do you feel your relationships struggle to get your attention?

3. Who do you identify with more—Mike or Mia? Why?

4. Wisdom defines play as an attitude that we can bring into our work, leisure and relationships. Think through the three parts of primary play (loving whatever we do, whomever we do it all with and for, and doing it all because an almighty Father is at work everywhere around us and in us making all things new). To what degree are you experiencing this "triple play" in your work, play and love? Choose one response: (1) not at all, (2) not much, (3) not sure, (4) pretty strongly, (5) very strongly. Write in a journal and/or share with someone the reasons for your answer.

chapter two

Play and Flow

Our search for balance and direction begins not with our call to a career but rather with our call to play. So says Lady Wisdom. But what does this mean in practical terms? Proverbs reminds me that the search for wisdom may take me to strange places. One of those strange places is gaming theory. If I want to bring more play into my life, to make room for this potent entity called primary play, then I need to look at the mavens of play and listen to what they have to say. In this chapter I converse with a few experts on play to see what we can learn in applying Proverbs 8 to the challenge of work-life balance. One is a medical doctor. One is a gaming theorist. One is a psychologist. All have important things to tell me about how to become a high-performance work-life "player."

Let me begin with the doctor. Stuart Brown, founder of the National Institute for Play, wrote in his bestselling book on play that "of all animal species, humans are the best players of all." Everything about us is "built to play and built through play."[1] He claims that in the modern world we have removed play from the general rhythm of life, reserving it for special, structured moments. Putting play into a silo has taken away much of the joy of life in general.

"Life without play," he writes, "is a life without books, without movies, art, music, jokes, dramatic stories. . . . Play is what lifts people out of the mundane." Brown goes so far as to call play a kind of "oxygen—it's all around us, yet goes mostly unnoticed or unappreciated until it is missing."[2] Isn't this emphasis on

Stuart Brown   Jane McGonagall   Mihaly Csikszentmihalyi

Game theory can help us become wisdom workers who practice the art of primary play

play irresponsible, suggesting that we should work less and just have fun? Brown says no. "We don't need to play all the time to be fulfilled," he writes. Play instead must be seen as a catalyst. "The beneficial effects of getting just a little true play can spread through our lives, actually making us more productive and happier in everything we do."[3]

According to Brown, play needs to be seen as an area of life on par with work and love. It also needs to be seen as an area that may refresh both work and love. Many emerging adults are stuck in the work hard–play hard rut. Brown calls us to bring play and playfulness into every area of life so that these beneficial effects of play (lifting us out of the mundane and putting delight back into daily life) can "spread through our lives." The implication of this is that play may well be the area that integrates all of life. The delight-driven nature of play is exactly what I need to help me work and love like Lady Wisdom; delight becomes the integrating center that brings my life into balance. Play, then, is as necessary as work and love to a balanced life because play has the potential to refresh and

Play is the oxygen of work and love

integrate these other areas. But how does that integration take place? Gaming theory offers some help.

Jane McGonagall believes gaming can change the world. She works as a research director for the Institute for the Future (IFTF) in Palo Alto, California, the world's oldest future-forecasting organization. One of the trends the IFTF has been tracking is the rise of a gaming culture in the West where tens of millions of people spend twenty hours a week living in virtual reality. How do we make sense of this trend? McGonagall uses an old trick when it comes to understanding trends and what they mean for our future. "To develop foresight, you need to practice hindsight."[4] This is not just her personal conviction, but it informs the work of the institute. She describes the IFTF mantra: "To understand the future, you have to look back at least twice as far as you're looking ahead." McGonagall has tracked the use of play to accomplish real-world change as far back as the time of Herodotus, the Greek historian. Herodotus wrote of King Atys of Lydia, who managed his people through a famine. His strategy? A massive, multiplayer game. The king organized the entire nation around a game of dice made out of sheep's knuckles. This gaming culture produced a national competition for eighteen years until the famine ended and life went back to normal.[5]

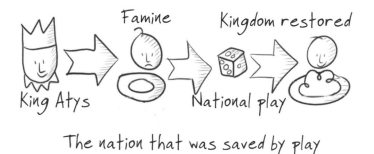

The nation that was saved by play

The gaming literature offers four principles that could transform work-life balance. The first principle of gaming theory is *form*. Most games—even those as wildly different as golf, the board game Scrabble or the video game *Halo*—have four basic elements. First, there is *a goal to pursue,* which defines how to win. Second, there is a *set of rules* that provide boundaries within which we must pursue that goal. Third, there is a *feedback system* that tells us whether we are making progress, accumulating points or beating the game. Finally, there must be *voluntary participation*. It isn't a game if we only play under protest.[6]

What would happen if I structured more of my life and work around these elements of a game? What if I defined a specific goal for my work on a daily basis? What if I set up some rules to help me focus on achieving that end (use a timer, keep lists, take frequent breaks)? What if I established a feedback system so that I would have a sense of progress, however small, during the

What makes a game a game?

Goals	Rules
Feedback system	Voluntary participation

The first principle of game theory is form

Flow happens when I am fully engaged with an external challenge

The second principle of game theory is flow

course of a day? And what if I approached my work like a volunteer rather than a slave or employee? What if I did it because I really wanted to? This is the principle of form.

The second principle of gaming theory that impresses me and seems to be transferable to work is the principle of *flow*. Many gaming theorists, including McGonagall, make liberal use of this concept, which originated with Mihaly Csikszentmihalyi, a pioneer figure in the new positive psychology movement.

His book *Flow: The Psychology of Optimal Experience* helped ignite the movement and remains one of the seminal studies in the field.[7]

Csikszentmihalyi defines flow as "the state in which people are so involved in an activity that nothing else seems to matter; the experience itself is so enjoyable that people will do it even at great cost, for the sheer sake of doing it."[8] Flow occurs when the challenge one is facing is exactly matched by the effort and energy expended. It is the moment when one feels fully alive. Time flies when you are experiencing flow.

Wisdom work is all about flow. When Lady Wisdom says in Proverbs 8 that every day she is playfully working, she is describing flow. Note, however, that flow is not to be confused with sheer willpower. Duty doesn't produce flow. Only delight does. Duty may be the brakes that keep me from heading in the wrong direction, but delight is the set of wings that bears me aloft, giving me a sense of freedom. Gaming theory helps one maximize flow by structuring daily life in the form of a game in order to produce that feeling of full engagement.

The third principle of gaming relevant to work-life balance is the concept of *fiero. Fiero* is an Italian word that means pride. This pride is not arrogance about oneself but exultation in a moment of triumph over adversity. It is the feeling generated by an "epic win." Jane McGonagall writes that though we "may not be able to define it exactly . . . almost all cultures show it the same way: We throw our arms over our head and yell."[9]

Christians talk about praise in the same way a gamer talks about *fiero*. When we experience, in and through God, an epic win, we want to lift our hands and shout. I would love to feel more of that in my areas of calling. I hardly know what a win would look like in some of my to-do items in a given day. I long for a feeling of "epic win" that would replace my lethargy and apathy with boredom-killing *fiero*.

The final principle of gaming theory with relevance for calling and balance is *fearlessness*. McGonagall writes about how gamers in massively multiplayer online (MMO) games like *World of Warcraft* don't fear dying in the game. They are willing to take risks because they know their avatar will be resurrected and

Fiero is the feeling of an "epic win"

Fearlessness is the freedom to fail and begin again

Fiero is the third principle of game theory

Fearlessness is the fourth principle of game theory

will have more power and experience points than before. Failure leads to future success for fearless gamers. "When we are experiencing flow," writes McGonagall, "we don't even mind if we fail." Instead, "when we do fall off, you feel the urge to climb back on."[10]

In a similar way, we may be optimistic about calling, career and future achievements when we are young, but at some point in life the "intimations of mortality" arise, saying to our soul, "Your time is up, it's time to move on." To which our heartfelt response is "Wait a minute, this can't be happening to me. I haven't even begun to live. Where are all the good times I was going to have?"[11] The antidote to being paralyzed by fear is fearlessness, that sense that we cannot ultimately die or fail. Fearlessness tells us to get up and get back in the game. When people are feeling flow in life, work and play, they feel free from fear. "The fact that one is not slim, rich, or powerful no longer matters. The tide of rising expectations is stilled; unfulfilled needs no longer trouble the mind. Even the most humdrum experiences become enjoyable." We are fearless.[12]

How do these four principles of gaming theory (form, flow, *fiero* and fearlessness) apply to our search for direction and balance in life? The first delight of Lady Wisdom's way of working is playful gladness in whatever we do. This is clearly a play dynamic. The form of a game demands doing something because I want to do it, not out of coercion. Gaming theory also suggests that I need to structure my work and to-do lists in ways that help me define what an "epic win" would look like in those areas. I also need to make a game out of the list, with rules and some kind of point system for feedback. Once I follow the lead of wisdom in turning daily life and work into the form of a game, the higher benefits experienced by gamers will be mine to enjoy.

I will begin to experience flow when I love what I'm doing so much that I don't want to stop. I will also begin to experience *fiero*. When I define my work and life each day in ways that tell me what a win would look like, I have a chance to work toward the exhilarating feeling of *fiero*. When I structure my work and life using the wisdom of gaming theory I will experience fearlessness. Play cannot take place in an atmosphere of danger and destruction. Bomb threats would empty out any stadium in the world, no matter how big the game. Only safety and security can create the ideal conditions for play. Lady Wisdom reminds me that I am never alone in my quest for work-life balance. Because a good and great God is with me and not against me, I have the power of fearless flow, a constant stream of playful delight in whatever I am doing and in whomever I am doing it all with and for.

McGonagall mentions one more insight from gaming theory that can help people improve real life—becoming *autotelic*. This is also a term from Csikszent-mihalyi. It refers to the ability to create the conditions for flow in your work quite apart from the circumstances or situation. No one gets a job where the boss greets you at the door every morning and tells you to have fun playing and flowing through the day. Our work is about performance. It is about productivity. It is about profit and pressure. I can't expect anyone else to bring the spirit of play into my work other than myself. To be autotelic is to create the conditions that will produce flow, fearlessness and *fiero*. And it is up to the individual, following Wisdom's call, to develop that creative power. Being a wisdom worker for the twentieth century means being autotelic—a gaming master who knows how to create the conditions for play no matter where I am or what I am doing.

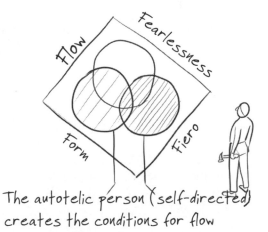

The autotelic person (self-directed) creates the conditions for flow

Of Tomatoes and To-Do Lists

After I learned about Proverbs 8 and understood how gaming theory could help me follow Lady Wisdom's call, I began looking for some practical ways to turn my daily life into a game where I could create the conditions of flow, *fiero* and fearlessness. My search led me to a tomato, or as the Italians say, a *pomodoro*. The pomodoro technique was created by an Italian graduate student named Francesco Cirillo in the late 1980s. It is quite simple but highly effective and is used the world over by students and business people alike. The key idea is doing one's work in increments of twenty-five minutes. No matter what is on the to-do list for a given day, everything is broken down into "pomodoros," the nickname given to the kitchen timers that graced many Italian kitchens back in the 1980s. The key is to race the clock in order to beat the timer. This simple game adds the element of playfulness to work that is essential for the wisdom worker. In proper pomodoro technique you keep completing tasks, with five-minute breaks between them and a longer break after so many consecutive tasks have been accomplished. I seldom practice the technique as rigorously as this, but I do make up my to-do list each morning (often the first thing I do each day), and then when I am ready to start, I click my timer (a digital version of the old pomodoro timer) and jump into the game of life. The timer is key. My timer has a loud tick (an important element in the technique) and immediately focuses my mind on the first task at hand. Beating the clock gives me my first *fiero* of the day. More importantly, the timer draws me into a state of flow that keeps me working even after the "ding" goes off. This is ultimately more valuable.

I have added an additional gaming element to the pomodoro technique. Every day I seek to accumulate at least ten tomatoes. This is my epic win. I get one point for every task I accomplish or any action that cannot be measured by a tomato. I don't put a timer on when I am spending time with my wife, Lois. I will often give myself a point when I am tempted to get irritated while in line at the supermarket or at another driver. By choosing to "play" rather than react, I experience more flow and fulfillment. Golf is one of my favorite games, so I

The pomodoro technique by Francesco Cirillo is a useful tool for creating flow in our daily life

use a golfing scoring system to help me visualize my points. Others may use football, soccer or even a role-playing game where your daily points enable you to advance to the next room, level or achievement.

Silly, isn't it? Why would someone reduce the important things that need to be done each day to ridiculous games and ticking tomatoes? Life is a serious matter, not a joke. I could not agree more. And that is why Lady Wisdom calls us to primary play in all of life. It works. And it works because Lady Wisdom— and the whole of the Bible—says it will. Anything that helps me to produce playful delight in the whatever, the whomever and the wherever is a welcome tool in the search for productive and balanced living.

The astute reader may be wondering how gaming my day helps with work-life balance. Maybe it helps me get more done, but does it help me integrate? Part of the value of making a game of the to-do list is the potential for integration. When I make my list each day I make sure to include play and love items as well as work. As I play the game of daily life, each of the three areas is given equal weight. I may have many more work items on the list than love or play items, but each category is worth the same value. Psychologically this frees me to put as much energy into play and love items as into work items. The result is a natural and daily work-life balance.

Balancing your to-do list helps
create work-life balance

I hear someone asking, politely, Am I not aware that work is a pain for most people and the opposite of play? How do I deal with the objection that work today makes this kind of playfulness impossible? Didn't Marx teach me anything about work as "alienating"? My immediate response is that the questioner is correct. Work today, for the vast majority of the world's people, seems to be "play proof." But that was never God's intention. To recover God's original playful design for work I would like to turn now to the early chapters of the book of Genesis.

Thinking It Through

1. Stuart Brown's research suggests that play may be the area of life that can balance and integrate all the rest. What evidence does he give for this? Do you agree or disagree?

2. Jane McGonagall argues that one can learn how to work and live by studying gaming culture and theory. What does she mean by using gaming concepts such as form in order to experience the emotional benefits of gaming?

3. Gaming theory describes the emotional highs of gaming in terms of flow, *fiero* and fearlessness. Define these key terms. What makes them so attractive for gamers? How would your work-life balance change if you could experience these three emotions consistently in your work life?

4. How does gaming theory link with what Proverbs 8 is teaching?

5. How might the pomodoro technique be a tool to cultivate flow, *fiero* and fearlessness into our daily life?

6. Wisdom not only changes the way we work, play and love, it also challenges our old stories—habits of thinking that often lead to stress and misery rather than flow and satisfaction. This is particularly true in the area of work. What kind of old narratives about work did you grow up with? Who shaped your view of work? What ongoing effect do these stories and individuals have on you today? As you analyze your old work stories, what are some features of

your work paradigm that need to be improved? How useful is the wisdom approach outlined above in offering new ways to think about our tasks?

Taking Action

1. Try a flow experiment.

2. Identify two items that you need to do today. It may be an errand to run, a homework assignment or an email to write. Decide how many twenty-five-minute work periods you will need to do these tasks. Keep it simple.

3. Using either a kitchen timer or a stopwatch on your computer, phone, tablet or watch, set the timer to twenty-five minutes and jump into the first task. Make sure you can hear the ticking noise if possible. Imagine a reward you will give yourself if you can do the task before the time expires. After the timer rings take a five-minute break and then do the next task until the two items are done.

4. Flow is the feeling of being fully engaged with the challenge at hand. It produces adrenaline as well as a higher degree of satisfaction from seemingly trivial activities. Did you experience any flow during this exercise? If so, what elements contributed to the adrenaline rush? Imagine being able to do many or most of your daily tasks in this state of flow. Did you feel any *fiero*? Rewarding yourself in small ways (five minutes of surfing the web, checking on sports teams or having a snack) for epic wins is a great way to cultivate the spirit of play that we need in every area of life.

5. After giving the pomodoro technique a spin, try adding other gaming elements to your work and life flow. One of the basics of "gamification" is cre-

ating a fun feedback system that gives you some idea of how you are doing. Daily life lacks these feedback systems, so the wisdom worker has to create them. Go through one entire day attempting to accomplish at least ten items on your to-do list using the pomodoro technique wherever appropriate. Pick a favorite sport or gaming metaphor in order to create the conditions for *fiero* and flow, whether it's scoring birdies, hitting home runs, accumulating happiness points or collecting epic win levels in a self-created role-playing game. As you wind up the day, think back and evaluate: to what degree did the gaming elements help reduce negative stress, increase focus and enhance productivity and balance? If this didn't happen, figure out what adjustments you need to make and try the experiment again tomorrow.

chapter three

The Eden Call to Work

Why do people work? Ridiculous question, really. Why do we eat or breathe? Necessity, survival, biological instinct all come quickly to mind. But work meets more than just basic human needs. Abraham Maslow's oft-quoted (and much criticized) "hierarchy of needs" suggests that we work for more reasons than mere survival. Maslow argued that the spectrum of human need went from survival to self-actualization. Later in his life he posited that our highest level of need, and therefore of satisfaction, is self-transcendence. Work has a role to play in every level of need, even the higher ones. One of the primary longings of emerging adults is for great work. They may insist that they work simply to make money, but in their heart of hearts they want work that satisfies their soul and makes the world a better place. For many young adults, that ideal view of work is frustratingly difficult to realize. Rates of unemployment and underemployment for recent college graduates are growing.[1]

The frustration we feel in work is not just limited to the tight job market. Issues of gender bias, corporate greed, bad bosses, underemployment, and fear of poverty and debt also fuel work angst. I'd like to look at a very basic belief our culture has about work and some of the deep frustration that belief generates.

The hierarchy of needs and the place of work

Maslow's need	I want work to be
self-actualization	place of creativity
esteem	my identity & worth
belonging	my "family," friends
security	parent who cares
physical needs	source of money

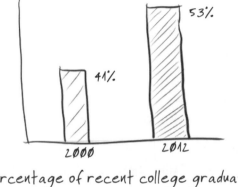

Percentage of recent college graduates unemployed and underemployed

Most young Americans have grown up with a very specific understanding of work. In conversations about what made America great or what will transform Third World economies, many experts point to the Protestant work ethic.

Hammered out in the controversies of the sixteenth-century Reformation by theologians like Martin Luther and John Calvin, the Protestant work ethic reached its most powerful expression in the Puritan movement in colonial New England. The heart of this work ethic is that the work we do for a living is the supreme act of worship. In the Middle Ages calling was understood as something that only religious people had. Monks, priests, nuns could be called, but the rest had to settle with a second-rate Christian life. Protestants turned the concept of calling on its head. They believed God's call to work covered all vocations, not just priests or monks. God's call to sell coffee or fish or bonds was a sacred act of worship for the committed follower of Christ. All work, therefore, was sacred, the Puritans proclaimed. Max Weber famously summarized the impact of this practical theology of work on the Western world and declared it the secret of the successful capitalism that brought wealth to Western shores.[2]

Max Weber saw the Protestant work ethic as the driver of Western capitalism

This Protestant view of work has been a powerful force in shaping our country. But what if renewing our call to work means doing some serious surgery on the Protestant work ethic? What if it means standing some of the conventional wisdom about work on its head? It is time not to retire the Protestant work ethic but to revitalize it by drinking deeply from the original call to work.

That call is found in the Bible's book of beginnings, Genesis:

> So God created mankind in his own image,
>> in the image of God he created them;
>> male and female he created them.

> God blessed them and said to them, "Be fruitful and increase in number; fill the earth and subdue it. Rule over the fish in the sea and the birds in the sky and over every living creature that moves on the ground." (1:27-28)

The call of wisdom takes place at the dawn of time, and the Eden call to work takes place soon after. Traditional views of work define it as "purposeful activity involving mental, emotional or physical energy or all three whether remunerated or not."[3] Technically there is nothing wrong with this definition. But describing work this way is like describing a Beethoven symphony as purposeful group-generated sound involving blowing, plucking and beating various mechanical instruments either for pay or not. It may be technically true, but it misses the soul of the activity.

Tim Keller gets closer to the soul of work when he points out that God's creative activity in Genesis, full of delight and originality, is described using the common Hebrew term for human work (*melakah*). Unlike other creation accounts in the ancient Near East, the work of creation described in Genesis was not an expression of cosmic warfare in which rival gods sought to outdo each other. In Genesis, "God makes the world not as a warrior digs a trench but as an artist makes a masterpiece."[4] God didn't have to work. For him, work had nothing to do with necessity, struggle or survival. Instead, he worked out of playful delight. God's work must then define our work. When he turns to our first parents and calls them to join him in the work of creation and culture building, he has something creative and positive in mind. Human work, in light of God's work, can be defined as "rearranging the raw material of God's creation in such a way

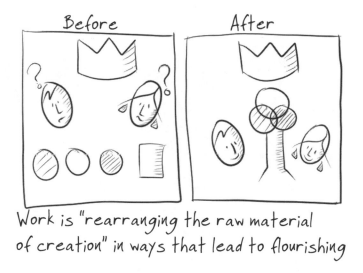

Work is "rearranging the raw material of creation" in ways that lead to flourishing

that it helps the world in general, and people in particular, thrive and flourish."[5] In its essence, work is creative and good, critical to human fulfillment. Work is playing creation with God. But sadly, this is not the primary view of work in our world today.

What the Call to Work Is Not

Why do most people see work so negatively when Genesis describes it in such positive light? A little history of work may shed light on the question. Aristotle and the ancient Greeks thought that work—at least manual work—was a curse. Work was "unleisure." Leisure was the purpose of life because it enriched and ennobled people. Work made them beasts of burden. Despite the best efforts of the Protestant Reformation to redeem work and turn it into something life enhancing and spiritual, the modern world has tended to default to Aristotle.[6]

Aristotle rejected manual work in favor of leisure

19th-century thinkers attacked the Protestant work ethic by removing its biblical basis

Modern thinkers as diverse as Adam Smith, Marx, Darwin and Freud all agreed that the Protestant work ethic was no longer sacred. For Smith, work was about generating profit. For Marx, work was alienation created by uncaring capitalists with cash registers for hearts. For Darwin, work was part of the struggle to survive. Freud saw work as the ego's attempt to find mastery and control in its environment. Common sense tells us work is more than these reductionist views. For many of us, however, the real-world experience of work supports the gloom and doom thinking of these masters of suspicion.

What Work Is: Performance

Genesis 1 contains none of this negative thinking about work. But if work in theory is about creative rearranging of the "stuff" of creation to bring about the flourishing of the world and of people, then how do we go about doing this practically? Let me suggest three key parts to understanding work as playing creation with God. The first part has to do with craftsmanship or performance. The second has to do with purpose. The third has to do with play. Let me start with the most obvious part of work: performance.

The first thing about work as performance is that whatever we do for work, either voluntarily or for pay, has to imitate God's work. He is not just going through the motions in Genesis 1. He is giving us a model and a map for our partnership with him. So how does God work? He makes things. He loves playing creation, bringing new things into existence out of nothing. And this is the key part of the original call to work. We can call this the performance principle of the call to work. It is about the craftsmanship that brings new things, things of beauty and utility, into existence.

The amazing thing about work as performance is that the norms of good work are very simple and pretty much the same, regardless of the type of work. They work whether you are writing computer code or running for public office. First is the norm of planning well. Second is doing well. Third is reviewing well.

Each of these rules is based on the way God worked in creating the universe. It came from his mind, so he planned it. He brought it into existence by his power; that's the "do it" rule. And he reviewed it; he looked at everything and delighted in its goodness. But he also created human beings to improve, enlarge and build upon what he made. Reviewing means evaluating our planning and performance in order to keep improving in our work.

I think about the area of teaching, the profession I know the best. To a large degree, good teaching is the result of good planning, good performance and good evaluation. In fact, the plan, do and review pattern can lead to improvement

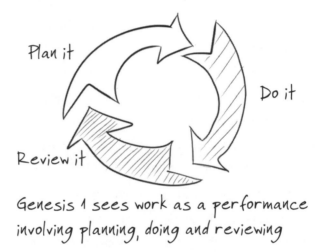

Genesis 1 sees work as a performance involving planning, doing and reviewing

in everything we do if applied correctly, whether painting, engineering or music. Good work is an iterative process that through trial and error creatively uses the raw material of God's creation to maximize human and environmental flourishing. God's norms for work would increase productivity and prosperity.

Which raises the question, aren't we still just talking about the Protestant work ethic when we talk about these norms of performance? Not exactly. Performance was one of the pieces the Protestant work ethic stressed. But it's missing some other important elements. Work is not just competence; it is effort that accomplishes certain purposes. That is norm number two.

What Work Is: Purpose

Performance—doing something well—is just one piece of the puzzle of renewed work. Doing something for a meaningful purpose is a second norm of the original call to work. What is God's great work in Genesis 1? Creating a universe? Partly. What excites the writer of Genesis, however, is not the vastness of heaven and earth but the beauty and utility of a single garden spot.

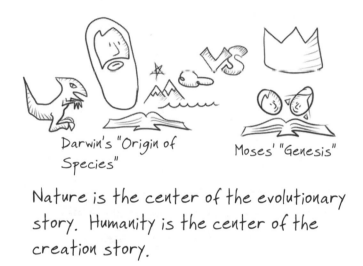

Darwin's "Origin of Species"

Moses' "Genesis"

Nature is the center of the evolutionary story. Humanity is the center of the creation story.

The purpose behind God's work is creating an Eden where humanity can dwell and grow. In the original call to work, God calls us to join him in this work by building little Edens everywhere. What do I mean by this? Eden work is about a meaningful combination of beauty and utility. Utility is doing that which leads to human flourishing. Beauty is surrounding the flourishing with wonder and order. When both are present, you have Eden work. Eden work is the mother who paints murals in the nursery as well as making sure it is antiseptic and safe. It is the policeman who really does protect and serve but also gets involved in the community. Eden work is the coffee shop that not only sells great coffee with a smile but has great atmosphere. It is the auto repair shop that is clean, efficient and honest. It might be the great basketball court in a housing project or the church on the corner that offers tutoring and support groups in a clean and welcoming space. It is the teacher who makes sure the school room is brightly lit, full of visuals and ordered for learning. It is the programmer who

Genesis 1 and the purpose of work:
building little Edens everywhere

codes well but doesn't use his skills to hack. It is supper time with lovingly prepared food, candles and great conversation. Beauty. Utility. Together they can build little Edens anywhere. This is the norm of purpose.

Beauty and utility make up one of the most stunning features of the creation. When we look at God's work in creation and explore his purposes, one of the stunning discoveries is the anthropic nature of creation. Most of us know what scientists mean by this term. The anthropic principle is the fact that the universe, for all its vastness, is perfectly structured to sustain human life on earth. The distance to the sun is ideal, for example. Closer and we burn up. Farther away and we freeze up. But how does this term relate to work?

In Genesis 1 we see that everything created from day one onward climaxes on day six with the creation of humans. God gets this beautiful house (earth) and farm (the garden) ready and then brings in the lucky couple who get to live there. Day seven is when God rests, his great work of creating humanity in a place of total beauty and utility done.

The purpose of work, however, is more than utility. Our work is for God as well. Not that he needs our labor. But he loves the work of his hands. Seven times in the story of creation God says that his work was "good." His work of making things gave him pleasure and had real utility. Work is not just humanistic in the sense of making humans the center of everything. We need to be God-centered but also focused on human flourishing, because that's how God works. Christian theology teaches that God is a Trinity of persons, a divine family of Father, Son and Spirit. This family of one God in three persons works supremely for the pleasure of his divine family but chooses to glorify himself by creating a paradise of plenty and prosperity for humanity, for others.

From this we learn that work needs to be theanthropic. That is, we need to make sure whatever we do leads to human flourishing and enhances human life. We also need to work in a way that doesn't treat God as the enemy but recognizes him as both the source and the ultimate goal of our work. We need to get beyond money, position or power as the driving motivations in our work. Those purposes burn us up. Working theanthropically builds us up.

When we work we must keep the end in view. This involves doing things that help people and not doing things that hurt them. That would be anti-work. At the same time our work must be something that God would approve of and delight in. But therein lies a tension. We can fall into the Promethean spirit of

Eden work delights in honoring God as the source of life even as we gladly meet the needs of others

work. Prometheus is the legendary Greek hero who stole fire from the gods in order to save mankind. The gods punished Prometheus for his act, even though it meant the survival of humanity. The point of the story is clear: humans are good; the gods are bad.

This Promethean DNA runs deep in all of us. When human needs and divine desires clash, we have a tendency to assume God is the enemy and humans the heroes. Instead we must work with God and not against him in whatever we do.

But how do we get rid of bad ideas about work? That brings us to the third norm of work: doing everything in the spirit of primary play.

Playful Work

Where can I find the primary play of Proverbs 8 in the story of creation? Where does it talk about the playful delight in whatever I do and whomever I do it with because wherever I look I see an almighty Father holding me in his arms and making all things new? On a quick reading it seems to be mostly farming work going on without much primary play. And while there is a command to work, there doesn't seem to be a command to play.

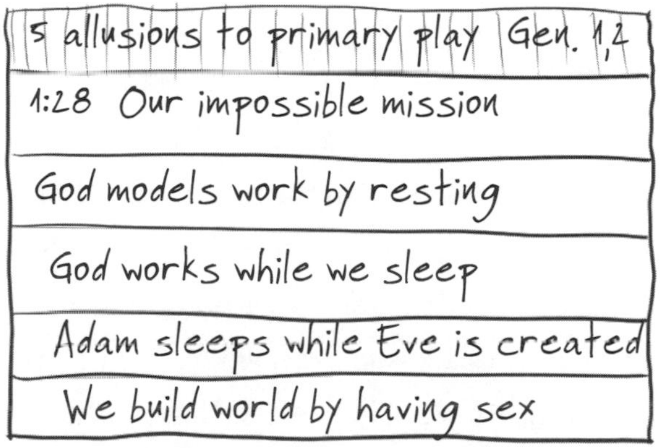

```
5 allusions to primary play  Gen. 1,2

1:28  Our impossible mission

God models work by resting

God works while we sleep

Adam sleeps while Eve is created

We build world by having sex
```

The third norm of work: primary play

But a closer reading tells another story. The third norm of playful work is woven throughout the first two chapters of Genesis. Let's look at five different ways God calls us to bring play into our work.

The first hint of primary play is in Genesis 1:28. Human beings are created. It is day one of their existence. They were made in God's image but have zero work experience. They open their eyes to a universe so vast, beautiful and breathtaking that it can only be a miracle to them. As they gaze at the miracle, the God of creation says, "Okay, I have a job for you right away. I want you to build a world just as I have." They must have smiled. So there's the first call to see work in a Proverbs 8 playful way: God makes everything. And two naked people, with a pretty empty résumé, get called to be his co-creators. This is funny.

But that's not all. Right after he tells them to be his partners in creation, what does he do? He rests. On day six he told them to change the world. If I am Adam and Eve, I would be watching carefully on day seven to see what that kind of work looks like. Day seven arrives. They are all eyes and ears, ready to take notes. So what does God show them about their work? He rests. He is not tired; but he has achieved his goal. He has created a place for his children to live and love, to work and worship. So he celebrates. He parties. He just enjoys his work. He dreams of the creation completed in the future when Eden spreads over the whole earth. But he does his resting and celebrating and dreaming before the watching eyes of children who are wondering how to go about their calling. In other words, the Sabbath was a lesson intended to teach humanity to work in a playful way, not a Promethean way. God's second lesson in how to work with him in his world is to party, to join him in celebrating and enjoying his permanent achievement. Resting in and with God becomes the key to working in his world.

The third way God calls us to bring primary play into our work is found in God's definition of a day. Evening and morning composed the first day. (This is why the Jewish day starts at night.) But why does this matter?[7] The workday, from God's perspective, started not when humans went to work but when he went to work. God's work of calling light into existence or whales into being began at night while humanity was sleeping. When they woke in the morning, the work didn't start. It was already rolling. God was at work. Humanity always works the second shift. The only kind of work we can do is to join a God who is already working, getting things started, doing the heavy lifting. We go to work with our Father every morning knowing that he wants us to do everything out of playful delight in that relationship.

Consider the fourth way God calls us to primary play. In Genesis 2 Adam has been called to work when the woman, the crucial work partner, arrives on the scene. But what is his role in this critical partnership for world building? He falls asleep. He doesn't have to work, because God is at work. Implication? We cannot work properly until we are in a state of worry-free rest in God and his goodness and power. That's part of what the spirit of play gives to us.

What's the final way God calls us to bring the spirit of play into our work? Our work, according to Genesis, is to be fruitful and fill the earth and rule it well. That means having offspring who can work the earth. But how do we fulfill that fundamental call to work? By play. We slip into bed with our wife or husband and we leap together in the ecstasy of love and play and pleasure. This play is the critical condition for fulfilling our work.

We are not called to be over-stressed, fragmented workers running around like crazy people. Instead we are to work as fearless players for the kingdom. The Eden work ethic then, with its norms of quality performance, theanthropic purpose and playful spirit, brings us back to the call of wisdom in Proverbs 8:30. The Eden work ethic is about learning to play at God's side as delighted and dependent children, full of the triple delight of the whatever, the whomever and the wherever.

Work can be frustrating. It is at the center of a great spiritual war between the old me that wants to play against God in creation and the new me that wants to play creation with God. In this war, there is not only a destructive spirit of work we are trying to avoid. There is also a playful and powerful new spirit of work we are trying to nurture.

The Greeks had another myth that captured this attitude of play as the key to redeeming work. It is the story of Penelope, wife of Ulysses, the hero of the *Odyssey*, Homer's second great epic poem. Penelope waited twenty years for Ulysses to return from the war with Troy. While he had his series of misadventures on the way home, she faced a number of challenges herself. She faced over one hundred suitors that wanted her to give up on her husband for dead and marry them so that her beauty and riches could be theirs.

Penelope served these evil suitors. She hosted them at great expense and without complaint. But in all her work of serving others, she never forgot the higher purpose of her work: to remain faithful to her husband. She told her suitors that as soon as she was finished with her tapestries, she would talk with them about their marriage proposals. So during the day she wove her beautiful tapestries with skill and purpose. At night, however, she undid her work. Each day she started over. Her playful work prevented her from being unfaithful to her beloved. She was willing to work in this way even though she didn't gain the satisfaction of a completed project because her weaving was being done for a higher purpose. She worked in a way that would honor her marriage and prepare for the return of her husband. When he finally returned, her playful work was rewarded. Ulysses defeated the evil suitors and resumed his marriage with his faithful Penelope.

Am I suggesting that we should work half-heartedly, never finishing our projects? Just the opposite. The story is a myth, but one with special meaning for us. We must work at our best in our lifetime. But we must never work under

She works for the one she loves

She meets human need

Her work is of high quality

Penelope work as a model of Eden work and primary play

the presumption that progress, achievement and meeting human need is all about us and all up to us. The evil suitors, who clamor daily for humanity made in the image of God to work either like slaves or like masters of the universe, are the voices of folly. They whisper that God is far away and that he may never return to us; we are on our own. So play against God in creation.

The Penelope principle speaks a different truth. We are to do our work as best we can but then offer it up to God for him to do with it as he will. We don't need to pretend it is all about us or all on our shoulders. We can delight in the doing without trying to dominate creation or control others. That's the spirit of playful work. We don't need our work to last forever. But we need to offer up what we do to the forever God and watch what he does with it. We love and serve the world daily, but we avoid the seduction and the stress of the twisted approach to work so prevalent in our world today.

Katherine Leary Alsdorf is a modern-day Penelope. She was a successful CEO in a promising technology company that was about to go public. One investment bank valued the potential IPO value of her company at 350 million dollars. She was also a new Christian struggling to understand how her faith related to her work. She describes what happened next. "After eighteen months of relentless work the company failed. We were part of the Internet bubble, and when it burst, it took us with it."[8] When she announced to her staff that the next day would be their last, they were shocked. And then they did something that shocked Katherine. They came in on the last day, for no pay, and celebrated. "They brought in musical instruments to play for one another," Katherine wrote, "or demonstrated the tai chi they taught in the evenings, and they laughed about fun times together."[9] If work was just about money, they should have been standing in the unemployment line. But real work is not just about money. It is about creating, collaborating and doing something wonderful and new. It is about meeting human need and using our gifts to make the world a better place. It is not about winning. It is about playing—high-performance playing. As Katherine concludes: "Eventually I came to see that day as a glimpse of God at work, doing what God does: healing and renewing and redeeming."[10] When Katherine got a call from Redeemer Presbyterian Church in New York City asking her to help them start a ministry to people in the marketplace, she said yes. In her work as the executive director of Redeemer's Center for Faith and Work, Katherine has discovered that wisdom work is not about conventional success but rather about letting God and his good news of new creation turn our work upside down.

I am reminded of the story of the boy in the Gospels who offered his loaves and fish to Jesus for the feeding of the five thousand. Jesus took the little and made it into something great. That is the Penelope principle I need in order to turn my work from frustration to flow. Let's hear again God's simple call to work in a Genesis 1:28 way. Let's learn to smile at God's gift of Eden work, where high performance, high purpose and a playful spirit enable us to pack a little paradise into our lunch bags every day.

Thinking It Through

1. On a scale of 1 to 10, with 1 being work as total misery and 10 being work as total joy, rate your feelings about your main work (student, employee, entrepreneur, professional or volunteer). What are the reasons for your rating?

2. Explore Genesis 1:28. In light of God's modeling of work, what do these verses teach about human work?

3. Both the sacred and secular versions of the Protestant work ethic have had a huge impact on our world. Draw a line down the middle of a piece of paper. In the first column list the positives of this work ethic. In the second column list the negatives. What do these two lists tell you about this work ethic and its strengths and weaknesses? How would an Eden work ethic overcome some of the limitations of the Protestant work ethic?

4. This chapter argues that we need to move from a twisted view of work (high control, it's all about me and all up to me) to an Eden ethic captured in the story

of Penelope. What does that struggle of control look like at the places you work (office, factory, church, home, school, street, etc.)? What is its downside?

5. How does Katherine Alsdorf's story illustrate some of the dynamics of playful work?

Taking Action

1. Using simple drawings (circles for people, arrows for events, and boxes for ideas or things), fill one sheet of paper with pictures that depict who or what has shaped your view of work the most. Be sure to label each picture. Are there any surprises as you analyze what you have drawn?

2. Interview at least two people you know about their work. What drives them? What role do playfulness and celebration have, if any, in keeping them productive or focused?

3. Using gaming theory practices from the last chapter (pomodoro technique, flow, *fiero*, form and fearlessness) structure your workday not around making money or earning the next promotion but around human flourishing. Spend one day executing the plan. Evaluate it in the evening. What worked? What didn't? How did this approach affect your attitude, productivity and relationships at work?

chapter four

The Broken Call

One common objection to this idea of high-performance play, of bringing the spirit of primary play into one's work, is that it is a nice sentiment but totally unrealistic. Wouldn't it be great, people say, if we really could follow the call of Lady Wisdom into a life of primary play? Unfortunately, they add, it can't work in the real world. My boss, my background, the system or life being the way it is makes the idea of integrating my life through high-performance play simply impossible. The skeptics have a point. In this chapter I want to look at the "real" world, how it offers resistance to a life of Proverbs 8 playfulness. So let's begin with the question, what is the "real world" out there?

Money, Sex and Power

Emerging adults have grown up watching the baby boomer generation, the generation born after World War II, the generation that wanted to change the world back in the 1960s. This is my generation. We marched against the war in Vietnam. We rode the freedom buses in Mississippi. Our troubadours like Bob

Dylan sang that through our efforts the "times, they are a changin'."

We were the change. And then the sixties ended with a crash. The Beatles broke up. Violence rocked America as militant groups tried to bomb their way to change. The "real" world took over. We failed. And in the wake of that failure, our calling to a new kind of work, a new kind of play and new kinds of love dissolved into a very different approach to life. Work became the scramble for money. Play become more extreme, drug fueled, sex crazed. Love ended in divorce, broken families and out-of-control children. We looked for ways to control the chaos, ways to obtain power over people.

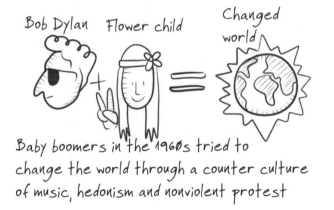

Baby boomers in the 1960s tried to change the world through a counter culture of music, hedonism and nonviolent protest

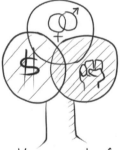

For many the pursuit of work, play and love became the quest for money, sex and power

My generation, however, was not the first to tumble from the heights of idealism to the rocks of reductionism. It is a problem as old as time. Let's take a look at the story behind this shriveled way of working, playing and loving. We start our search for answers in Proverbs once again.

Dame Folly's Call

Just as Lady Wisdom calls us to a life of kingdom play in Proverbs 8, so another lady calls us in the next chapter of the book. Proverbs 9:13-18 tells us who she is and what she wants:

> *Folly is an unruly woman;*
>   *she is simple and knows nothing.*
> *She sits at the door of her house,*
>   *on a seat at the highest point of the city,*
> *calling out to those who pass by,*
>   *who go straight on their way,*
>   *"Let all who are simple come to my house!"*
> *To those who have no sense she says,*
>   *"Stolen water is sweet;*
>   *food eaten in secret is delicious!"*
> *But little do they know that the dead are there,*
>   *that her guests are deep in the realm of the dead.*

Dame Folly, like Lady Wisdom, issues a call. This call is loud; everybody—even the busy passers-by—seem to take notice. Lady Wisdom shouts in the city and people carry on with their business. Dame Folly bellows and people listen. What is her call? Why is it so popular? Dame Folly can be easily paraphrased. "Don't think about life, but do what you feel like doing" ("let all who are simple come," v. 16). No wonder everybody listens. It's an easy call to respond to: Do it your way. Take whatever you want from life. Break the rules. Don't let your conscience get in the way. Forbidden fruit is the best kind. You only live once. The people love it.

Dame Folly's call, like Lady Wisdom's, can be summarized as a call to play, but a defiant one:

1. Delight in whatever is defiant ("Stolen water is sweet")

2. Delight in others who are defiant ("All who are simple")

3. Delight in doing it all as a way to defy death ("little do they know that the dead are there")

This call is to a kind of deadly play. It risks real work, play and love for the pleasure of defiance and doing things "my way." This call matches up well with the hedonism and expressive individualism of the modern world. What it lacks in virtue it claims to make up in realism. Death is the last bell for everyone. Grab life while you can. Defiance is the only tree that lasts in a realistic world. The tree of folly looks like this:

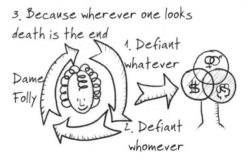

The defiant play of Dame Folly turns work, play & love into a fight for money, sex & power

We need to learn more about this fascinating character Dame Folly. What is her story? What does her call to defiant play mean? What are the consequences of following her call?

Dame Folly's Birth: Genesis 3 and the Call of Deadly Play

In Genesis 3 we read about the birth of Dame Folly in the fall of Adam and Eve. God had given them a particular call to help them develop discernment and trust. They were to eat of every tree except the forbidden tree, the tree of the knowledge of good and evil. This tree was good, as was all of God's creation, but they were not ready for it. The call of wisdom would have led the first humans to delight not only in whatever they were doing but also in doing it all under God's loving eyes and in his arms. This is the playful partnership with God that is at the heart of Lady Wisdom's call to play. The spirit of Dame Folly appears in the form of a serpent and issues the call of Proverbs 9: "Don't listen to your conscience and God. Do what you feel like doing. Grab what you want. Don't let God spoil the party. Nothing bad will happen." As a result, death enters human history.

God confronts the new disciples of folly and hands down the just verdict: you will experience the curse of folly and death in all of life. In a nutshell, the curse of sin is a life of primal fear: fear of God that makes us run away from him; fear of one another that makes us defensive and closed; fear of work because it now resists our planning, doing and reviewing; fear of intimacy because it will turn into a power struggle; fear of childbearing, for it will mean pain; fear of nature, for it will be cruel. Over all these fears is the fear of death. A voice deep within whispers even in the moments of our greatest happiness and achievement, "You will lose it all."

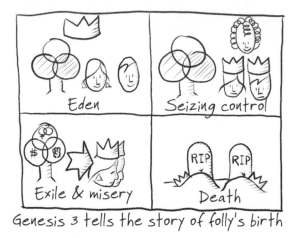

Genesis 3 tells the story of folly's birth

The call of wisdom embedded in creation is now lost. The loud call of folly has drowned out the sweet music of that first call. What does this mean? Living a life driven by primal fear means that:

1. *Delight in whatever we do is impossible.* Fear produces misery in whatever we do. We only feel alive when we are in rebellion. We feel most delight when we do the forbidden.

2. *Delight in whomever we do it with and for is impossible.* Delight in others is broken. We cannot trust them. We become addicted to doing what we feel like doing, impulsive people who grab without thinking and are slaves to our passions.

3. *Doing it all out of delight in a loving and almighty Father working everywhere around us to make all things new is impossible.* We are now afraid of God, and we construct alternative concepts of god to mollify our fears of judgment and divert our attention from our own twisted soul. We live in fear, the

shadow of death shrouding all of our work, play and love. Work-life balance is thrown into chaos.

Such is the effect of Dame Folly's arrival. Where has she gone since this opening chapter of her tragic story? One place is into our heads. So let's talk for a moment about Dame Folly's brain.

Playful delight in what I do → Fear & defiance in whatever I do

Playful delight in others → Fear of others

God at work everywhere → Fear of death all around me

Folly turns wisdom's triple delight into triple fear

Dame Folly's Brain: The Ten Deadly Thoughts

Most of us have never met Dame Folly directly, but we hear her voice in our heads frequently. She loves planting seeds in the rich soil of our minds. But her seeds are deadly, and her harvest, a horror. Theologians call them deadly sins. The original list of seven (or possibly eight) deadly sins was drawn up by the fourth-century Syrian holy man St. Evagrius, who called them deadly thoughts, not sins. He recognized that folly had implanted within us cognitions that can cripple us, hold us back from being fully alive and thwart the satisfying life of playful flow. What are these brain banshees that haunt our work, play and love?

Evagrius's list is slightly different from mine. Let me briefly comment on my digest of inner demons.

Pride. We know that pride is supposed to be the worst sin of all, but we don't always know why. Pride is more than just having a big head; it's more like having two heads. The first head of the monster has to do with our negative thoughts of God. This is the deadliest of all because it is the deepest of all and the hardest to remove. The first head of pride whispers to me that God is the problem and humanity is the solution. If God is allowed into our life, then no place is safe, no plan protected, no love secure.

The second head of pride whispers that most, if not all, people are minions of God seeking to destroy my life, frustrate my happiness and take away my freedom. This second head of pride is a backhanded recognition that people are made in the image of God and may still be on his payroll. When the worm of pride drills through my brain and heart, it kills my capacity to love. I can't love God, not the real God of the Bible at least. God is the enemy. I can't love others, not real people at least and not for long. They are, after all, God's spies and assassins. Pride must walk alone.

Lust. If God is the enemy and people are out to get me, then I am the only one left to care for my happiness. I am an orphan that must steal to eat. No one else can be trusted. Grabbing what I want when I want it becomes instinctive and uncontrollable. Lust, like pride, makes love impossible because love is offered as a gift, but lust sees all gifts as Trojan horses sent to cheat and enslave me. Only what is grabbed can be good.

Unbelief. If God is the enemy, then whatever he speaks cannot be trusted. I have a deep bias against anything that claims to be his word and a deep suspicion of those who claim to represent his truth. I am suspicious of absolutes for they remind me of he-who-cannot-be-named. I seek shelter behind a relativism that won't bind me and arbitrary absolutes that support my independence.

Greed. Greed messes with my head daily. If lust is a destructive appetite for satisfaction and pleasure, then greed is a destructive appetite for security and prosperity. These are good things to seek in and of themselves. By twisting the knife of fear, however, Dame Folly creates a panic for more that no amount of security and money can satisfy. And if God is my enemy, then I can't ever be secure. Greed is the search for peace gone crazy.

Anger. If God is the enemy, then I know who to blame when my will is thwarted, my self-esteem wounded or my rights violated. I must rage against him or his minions. I must fight those who oppose me and bring them down.

Fear. If God is the enemy, then I have a right to be paranoid. Every conversation could be a trap. Every stranger is a secret agent sent to subvert the sovereignty of the self. Every sky above me, real or imagined, is about to fall. Every promise of love and loyalty is about to be betrayed.

Bitterness. If God is the enemy, then everything is poisoned. He ruins everything. Every time I try to get ahead, he blocks the way. Every time I try to rise up, he knocks me down. Every good thing that happens, he takes it away. His very existence makes my happiness impossible, my dreams unreachable. He and his deluded champions have caught me in a web of misery and I cannot escape.

Self-pity. If God is the enemy, then I am wounded. There is nothing to be done against the cosmic bully except rage against him. I fought my best but have been stabbed and defeated by the enemy, bound in chains and thrown into a dungeon of lost dreams for which there is no key.

Sloth (or acedia). If God is the enemy, then why struggle or fight? Why care? Why try if, in the words of *Les Misérables,* "nothing ever changes, nothing ever will"? Sloth is more than laziness. It is nihilism. Nothing matters. Nothing has meaning. Nothingness is all. "No need to get excited . . . [for] life is but a joke," says Dylan's thief in "All Along the Watchtower." Better to spend my life on trivia, games or reckless pleasure than make the mistake of playing hard at the game of life. Why bother?

Despair. If God is the enemy, then there is no hope; there is no reason to live. The final reality is death and dark night. To quote Dylan again: "There is no way out of here."

No one I know thinks this way consciously, or at least not most of the time. But the point is that these thoughts lie deeply buried in our psyche and attack at key moments.

These deadly thoughts create a dramatic plot in our lives. The first four (pride, lust, unbelief and greed) lead to act one: rule. We don't trust God or others so we try to seize control, to become the one who calls the shots. This creates resistance and opposition from others who are trying to do the same thing. Act two results: rage. We fight against anything that stands in our way. During this stage we alternate between anger, fear and bitterness. The final act in the drama is ruin. Self-pity convinces me I am the victim rather than the responsible party. Sloth tells me to stop trying because God or others will just ruin and frustrate my plans and efforts anyway. Despair tells me that death is the only reality, and to wait for, or even hasten, that dire end.

Are only some filled with these and other negative thoughts? Are only some alienated from God and from the spirit of kingdom play? The Bible says that "all have sinned and fall short of the glory of God" (Romans 3:23). Translation? Everyone is in the mess that folly's call has inflicted. No one is experiencing the full life God intended for us in Genesis 1–2, and we are so addicted to folly that, left to our own devices, we will never find our way out.

Pride	God and others are enemy
Lust	only what is grabbed is good
Unbelief	God cannot be trusted
Greed	lust for security
Anger	fight for control
Fear	everything will fail
Bitterness	everything is poisoned
Self pity	everyone is against me
Sloth	why bother or care?
Despair	everything ends in death

My ten deadly thoughts

Rule ⟶ Rage ⟶ Ruin

The deadly thoughts create a certain dramatic plot in one's life. Pride rules but failure leads to rage and then finally resignation and internal ruin. One can play out this drama in a day, a season or a life.

Dame Folly's Box: Eden Ruined

The Greeks tell the story of Pandora. She was a given a box by the gods that she was forbidden to open. But open it she did, and all the evils of mankind were released by her disobedient act. Only hope was left inside and sealed for good. Dame Folly's birth opened her own particular box of horrors on our world and on our calling. Let me summarize the furies of folly's box under the acronym of EDEN. Folly brings about humanity's exile from Eden, the place of playful work, play and love, into a social, physical, spiritual, political and cultural wilderness where the original Eden gets inverted and distorted. Folly's public impact means Earth ravaged, Delight distorted, *Ekklesia* subverted and the Nations enslaved.

Earth ravaged. Humanity was called to turn the world into a garden of delight and beauty, just as God had done in Genesis 1. Dame Folly introduced a new twist. Humanity has declared war on the environment, raping and ravaging the earth in pursuit of money, pleasure and power. The deadly thoughts of pride and lust thus have political implications.

Delight distorted. Dame Folly calls us to turn our delight away from everloving eyes and arms and, in light of death and the grave, to "lick the earth," in Augustine's startling phrase. The only delight, the only kind of play possible in a world in which God is dead to us is the worship of creation itself rather than the Creator. Idolatry becomes epidemic.

Ekklesia *subverted*. *Ekklesia* is the Greek word for those who are called. The call of wisdom produces a new kind of people, those who delight in all of life, all work, play and love, all with and for God. Folly subverts this call and produces a different kind of people: those who revel only in defiant deeds, defiant relationships and the illusion that they are defying death. The followers of folly

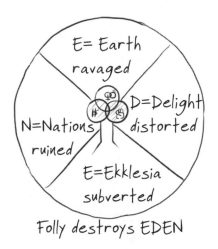

Folly destroys EDEN

cannot fix the world. They may speak loudly of saving the earth, healing the nations and finding happiness, but the deadly thoughts within produce disappointing and often disastrous results in practice.

Nations enslaved. Folly's box produces political, social, economic and cultural evils as well. The deadly thoughts in our mind and heart produce broken systems and institutions in the public sphere. Racism, corruption, poverty, disease and idolatry are but a few of the furies that have escaped folly's little box of horrors and brought misery to millions.

Folly and the Balanced Life

So we come back to the objection with which we started. This business of kingdom play and its triple delight seems like a nice idea, but it just doesn't work in the real world where the forces of folly have created a jungle in which only the fittest or the most ruthless and aggressive survive. There is no place for primary play in the jungle.

Dame Folly's call helps explain why the circles of work, play and love often seem to end up becoming twisted into money, sex and power. Folly creates a reductionist downdraft that pulls the leaves of calling from the tree of life to the ground. Primary play gives way to the ruthless play of defiance. Work-life imbalance is just one external symptom of how deeply broken humanity really is.

I grew up in a home in which the family faith was the American dream of money and power. There was no time for church. My father was a child of the Depression who grew up in abject poverty on a potato farm in northern Maine. He eventually became a lumberjack, working long days in the woods cutting timber. After a brief stint in World War II he returned to the lumber industry, but this time as an owner. He loved hard work and eventually made his million. The family was flush. We had a private plane that we took on vacations. We had a second home at the lake. We moved into a new home. But folly played heavily on the family. My workaholic father was a driven man, full of pride, greed and anger. These qualities drove his marriage to the breaking point. Something was clearly missing in the family soul. A series of reversals culminating in our house burning down broke folly's grip on my family. Lady Wisdom fought back. My father's dramatic encounter with God in midlife broke the hold of money, sex and power on our entire family and changed our direction forever. But it was a close call.

If Dame Folly's box has been unleashed, why is life still pretty good? Why are there beautiful sunsets, great teachers, good doctors, golf courses, winning teams, happy families, great friends and simple pleasures? The answer, not surprisingly, is that the calling and campaign of folly has not gone unopposed. God has started a resistance movement against EDEN ruined. Where and how that started and what it means for work-life balance is the next part of our story.

Thinking It Through

1. Read again the description of Dame Folly's call in Proverbs 9:13-18. How much does modern advertising echo this call and its summary (defiant action, defiant allies, defiant illusions)?

2. The chapter suggests that Dame Folly's birth means that the most basic emotion in life is fear. Do you agree or disagree? Give reasons and examples for your answer.

3. As you think through the deadly thoughts mentioned above, which ones haunt you most? What are some of the negative thoughts that stick in your head and compromise your joy and happiness? How have these thoughts affected your work? Your play? Your love?

4. "The deadly thoughts in our mind and heart produce broken systems and institutions in the public sphere." Do you agree or disagree with this statement? Why or why not? What light does James 4:1-3 add to the question? Take a look at some headlines and make some connections between our internal state and the external world.

5. How do you see folly's mission of EDEN ruined working itself out in your home, job, school, nation, city or people group?

Taking Action

1. Read the Walter Isaacson biography of Steve Jobs or watch the movie. Jobs is an interesting study in the struggle for work-life balance as well as in the pull of wisdom and folly in our own self-understanding and relationships with others. How does Jobs deal with the tension between running Apple for money and power on the one hand and running it in solidarity with friends and trusted colleagues on the other? How do these competing visions of work, play and love (which we are ascribing to wisdom and folly) shape his destiny? What does Jobs learn about himself and about leadership after returning to power at Apple in the late 1990s? To what degree does Jobs's eventual success at Apple justify his leadership style? Should he be considered a model of work-life balance?

2. Do a personal life balance audit using a SWOT analysis. This kind of analysis asks you to brainstorm about Strengths, Weaknesses, Opportunities and Threats. As you think about the war between wisdom and folly going on in our lives, what are some of the internal weaknesses (folly's deadly thoughts) you need to deal with, some resources you need to draw on and some threats around you to avoid?

chapter five

The Abraham Call to Believe

If folly is on the loose undermining the wisdom worker model of work, play and love, then what can we do to get our life back? The most important change needs to be at the "wherever" level of Proverbs 8. The only way I can playfully delight in whatever I am doing and whomever I am doing it all with is by removing fear from my life. This happens by learning to see God at work wherever I look. I need to get rid of folly's blinders so that I can see an almighty and all-loving Father at work everywhere around me and in me making all things new. If I don't see that, the whatever and the whomever falls apart. And if that falls apart, the best model I know of for work and life balance falls apart. The problem is that folly has so poisoned my thinking that I am blinded to the idea of God as almighty Father and to his active presence. God may be there, but folly whispers daily that such a God cannot be trusted and is useless for daily living.

New research indicates that Dame Folly's influence has been extensive. Christian Smith, in a series of well-researched and highly regarded studies on the spiritual and religious lives of American teenagers and twentysomethings, describes the prevailing view of God as "moralistic, therapeutic deism."[1] This is the belief that God exists, but not in a way that intersects with our daily life in any meaningful way (the deistic element); that he probably has some rules, although no one seems to agree on what they are (the moralistic element); and that he certainly wants me to be happy and do my thing (the therapeutic element). When God is seen through this lens there are real-life consequences. People end up living in a "morally insignificant universe," argues Smith.[2] He elaborates:

> People living in such a universe find themselves in a small corner of that empty space in which their short lives have come by chance . . . in a galaxy destined for extinction. There is no Creator who set humanity here and guides our lives and history with Providence. . . . In such a universe one's decisions and actions may indeed have certain pleasurable or painful consequences, but they have no particular meaning, purpose or significance beyond that.[3]

It doesn't take much imagination to see that the wisdom work model of life balance from Proverbs 8 is not possible in a morally insignificant universe emceed by a moralistic therapeutic deity. There is no almighty Father. There are no everlasting arms of love. There is no purposeful new creation going on all around me. Without the stimulus of a loving cosmic Creator we cannot respond with playful delight in all of life. I can only play when I am safe, and there is no way I am safe in a morally insignificant universe virtually abandoned by an absentee god.

That is where the call of Abraham comes to the rescue. I want us to listen in on some of his key conversations with his Maker. These conversations are a gateway to getting work, play and love back into balance by building a new sense of cosmic beauty and security.

Researcher Christian Smith calls
the dominant American view of God
"Moralistic Therapeutic Deism" in which
God is absent, just wants us to be happy,
but expects a certain basic morality

Abraham's Call

Abraham's call is found in Genesis 12:1-3, when our hero was still called Abram:

> The LORD had said to Abram, "Go from your country, your people and your father's household to the land I will show you.

> *"I will make you into a great nation,*
>   *and I will bless you;*
> *I will make your name great,*
>   *and you will be a blessing.*
> *I will bless those who bless you,*
>   *and whoever curses you I will curse;*
> *and all peoples on earth*
>   *will be blessed through you."*

Here we see God's response to the call of folly. He plans to remove it and promises to replace it with paradise once more. And he wants to use Abraham and his offspring to do so. Abraham's call is to believe in the mission of God, and it involves three elements: accepting God's new mission, leaving folly's old mission and playing for the Father in all of life.

Believing in the Mission of God: Accepting God's New Mission

Let's start with accepting. God announces that he has a major new project, one that seems to be as big and important as creation itself in Genesis 1.

Folly tells us that God is the problem and that humanity is the solution. But God tells us the opposite. The word "blessing," from the Hebrew word *berakah*, gives a glimpse of the solution to the problem of folly and its miseries. The English word "blessing" has been all but stripped of meaning. Today it means little more than saying a prayer before meals or feeling warm and fuzzy at a church service. Not so in Jewish culture, or African culture, for that matter, where the Swahili word *baraka* (which I will now use) echoes the original Hebrew meaning. When God brings *baraka* it means he will destroy all that is evil and wrong in the world and restore all that is right and good and that leads to human flourishing. *Baraka* means all things are made new.

So God announces to a listening Abraham that he is initiating some kind of *baraka* mission. Folly's call eventually led to EDEN ruined: an earth ravaged, delight distorted, *ekklesia* subverted and the nations ruined. By implication, God's project will lift the curse and replace it with blessing. Ever since Genesis 3, where folly's call to sin and death enter the world and our call gets broken into

Baraka (bless) means God will
lift the curse of sin and death and
make all things fully alive again

a thousand fragments, God has been preparing to do something about it. What does it involve?

God's mission can be summarized by once again using the acronym EDEN.

Earth restored. Sin and death have cursed the earth. Work is now a struggle between human abuse and exploitation of the earth and the proper development needed for humanity and nature to flourish. God's *baraka* mission will bring both human development and environmental renewal.

Delight renewed. Sin brought not just bad behavior but something more sinister and destructive: idolatry. We worship created things rather than the Creator; our delight is now misplaced, shifted to things in creation, like power, sex, politics, addictions, money, family, work. We were made to live and work knowing we are safe in God's arms, and instead our broken souls find him dull, distant and even revolting. One day, however, because of God's *baraka*, because he is on the EDEN mission, delight in him will be renewed and we will be restored to kingdom play completely.

Ekklesia, *the church, perfected.* "All nations will be blessed through you," God says to Abraham. The church is to be inclusive. Every ethnicity, nationality and cultural group without exception is to be part of the new called-out people of God. Under the rule of folly, the people of God are marginalized and irrelevant. Under God's mission, all that changes. His mission includes bringing all nations into his *ekklesia*.

Nations healed. All the misery, injustice, poverty, misrule and war that has ripped our world apart will come to an end. Shalom, the total peace and harmony of all of life, will be restored. In Revelation 22 God uses the leaves of the tree of life to heal the nations. This is one of his main *baraka* goals and is the climax of the EDEN project.

God's Mission is EDEN regained

Am I reading too much into these few verses from Genesis 12? Does it really set God's agenda for the rest of the Bible and human history? According to Old Testament scholar Christopher Wright, the scope and significance of this passage cannot be overestimated. "The call of Abram," affirms Wright, "is the beginning of God's answer to the evil of human hearts, the strife of nations and the groaning brokenness of his whole creation." In God's call to Abraham "a new world, ultimately a new creation, begins."[4]

One of the most amazing features of God's mission is that he wants us, heads and hearts still spinning from folly's call, to become his partners in making all things new. "All peoples on earth will be *baraka*-ed because of you." How do we partner with God in this mission of EDEN regained? Accepting his mission is the first step. But there is another crucial step.

Believing in God's Mission: Leaving

We not only have to accept that the heart of human life is a new partnership in the mission of God. We also need to sever the old partnerships of folly. God's mission is a direct response to the Babel project of Genesis 11. A centralized government rejects God's call to fill the earth by trying to keep everybody in one location. The people raped the resources of the earth to build a tower to God so that they could make a great name for themselves. This is the broken call of Genesis 3 taken to civilization-wide proportions.

And at the heart of the Babel project is folly's great assumption: that God is the biggest problem in life and humanity is the solution. God is far away. He is silent. He is indifferent to human need. He cannot be reached. God has abandoned us and we are on our own. But we can fix anything. We can restore Eden by building cities. We can regain delight by creating religion and achieving amazing feats and inventing wonders. We can create an *ekklesia* of uniform citizens under the control of a central authority to show how great our civilization is. We can heal the problems of the nations by becoming bigger and better. That's the Babel mentality. Self-reliance. Personal glory.

Believing God's mission means leaving behind the Babel mentality of self-reliance and self-glory

Abraham had to leave the Babel mentality of self-centeredness, self-reliance and self-glory behind. He had to shift from the lie that God is the problem and humanity is the solution to the truth that humanity is the problem and God is the solution. It took him his entire life to learn to play for the kingdom like that.

Believing in God's Mission: Playfully Living in the "Wherever"

The third element of the call to believe in the mission of God is the task of playing.

Playing for God's mission of EDEN regained means holding on to God and his work of new creation no matter what happens. It means letting his promises, power and beauty sink into us like sunlight into a leaf. It means seeing him at work around us making all things new and playfully partnering with him in our work, play and love. Throughout the rest of Abraham's life he would struggle mightily to hang on to the promise of God's *baraka* project in the face of counterevidence. The culmination of his struggle to believe God is at work everywhere around him, the critical condition for the restoration of playful partnership, comes in one of the final acts of Abraham's life.

Some time later God tested Abraham. He said to him, "Abraham!"

"Here I am," he replied.

Then God said, "Take your son, your only son, whom you love—Isaac—and go to the region of Moriah. Sacrifice him there as a burnt offering on a mountain I will show you."

Early the next morning Abraham got up and loaded his donkey. He took with him two of his servants and his son Isaac. When he had cut enough wood for the burnt offering, he set out for the place God had told him about. On the third day Abraham looked up and saw the place in the distance. He said to his servants, "Stay here with the donkey while I and the boy go over there. We will worship and then we will come back to you."

Abraham took the wood for the burnt offering and placed it on his son Isaac, and he himself carried the fire and the knife. As the two of them went on together, Isaac spoke up and said to his father Abraham, "Father?"

"Yes, my son?" Abraham replied.

"The fire and wood are here," Isaac said, "but where is the lamb for the burnt offering?"

Abraham answered, "God himself will provide the lamb for the burnt offering, my son." And the two of them went on together.

When they reached the place God had told him about, Abraham built an altar there and arranged the wood on it. He bound his son Isaac and laid him on the altar, on top of the wood. Then he reached out his hand

and took the knife to slay his son. But the angel of the Lord called out to him from heaven, "Abraham! Abraham!"

"Here I am," he replied.

"Do not lay a hand on the boy," he said. "Do not do anything to him. Now I know that you fear God, because you have not withheld from me your son, your only son."

Abraham looked up and there in a thicket he saw a ram caught by its horns. He went over and took the ram and sacrificed it as a burnt offering instead of his son. So Abraham called that place The Lord Will Provide. And to this day it is said, "On the mountain of the Lord it will be provided."

The angel of the Lord called to Abraham from heaven a second time and said, "I swear by myself, declares the Lord, that because you have done this and have not withheld your son, your only son, I will surely bless you and make your descendants as numerous as the stars in the sky and as the sand on the seashore. Your descendants will take possession of the cities of their enemies, and through your offspring all nations on earth will be blessed, because you have obeyed me." (Genesis 22:1-18)

Abraham wanted to delight in the security of a God who was going to bring life, not death, a God who was the solution and not the problem. But it was a struggle. God had announced that he wanted Abraham—and all who followed him in accepting his mission, leaving folly and playfully partnering with him—to be agents of EDEN regained. He needed to liberate Abraham from lingering elements of the Babel mentality by striking at the very root of the mentality, folly's insistence in Proverbs 9 that death and the grave are the final realities. Abraham gets it. He is willing to sacrifice Isaac, the son of blessing, and without succumbing to quiet rage or silent despair. In the New Testament book of Hebrews we are told that Abraham was acting out of a *baraka* mentality, not a Babel one. We read: "By faith Abraham, when God tested him, offered Isaac as a sacrifice. He who had embraced the promises was about to sacrifice his one and only son, even though God had said to him, 'It is through Isaac that your offspring will be reckoned.' Abraham reasoned that God could even raise the dead, and so in a manner of speaking he did receive Isaac back from death" (Hebrews 11:17-19).

Abraham believed in the mission of God, and in the God of that mission, to the extent that he trusted the *baraka* of resurrection would triumph over the curse of death. God is on a mission to see EDEN regained, and he calls us to join him in his work. But the first task is the Abraham call to believe in that kind of mission and in that kind of God.

Abraham's faith meant that he began to live and work like a much-loved child, like the wisdom worker of Proverbs 8:30-31. He began to delight in what he was called to do, to delight in those he was called to serve and to do it all secure in the God of *baraka*.

The mission of God always ends in life

I caught a glimpse of this playful partnering with God even in the face of death when my father passed away. He had been a pastor in Portland, Maine, at a small Congregational church. The church never reached the goals that my father had set for it. Numbers were small. Change was slow. Epic wins were few. But one of the greatest encouragements to him in all his years of ministry was the conversion of a troubled youth named Steve. Steve was from a rough background. God met him one day much like he met Abraham, and he sought out my father for spiritual guidance. My father talked with him about how to become a child of God through faith in Jesus Christ, and Steve's life changed. He graduated from high school and went off to college to study for the ministry. After college Steve became a pastor in a seaside town in midcoast Maine. His church flourished. Every year Steve invited my father to come and preach. He would always tell his congregation the story of how my father had "led him to the Lord." Even after my father retired, the yearly invitations and annual honoring continued. I can't think of anything in my father's pastoral ministry that gave him more joy and satisfaction than Steve's success.

And then one year there was no invitation. Steve had been fired from his church as a result of immorality and had left the ministry entirely. My father took the news hard. It was a crushing blow. My father's greatest achievement became his greatest disappointment. Then my father died.

It was a gray and overcast day when we laid his remains in a small cemetery in Union, Maine. I read a few words from Revelation 21 about the new heavens and the new earth and the death of death. It seemed like quite a distant hope at that moment. Few turned up for the burial, but there was a face I didn't recognize standing at the edge of the small gathering.

We concluded the burial and began heading toward the cars. The stranger stopped me and introduced himself. "I'm Steve," he said. He went on to tell the story not only of his moral failure but of how God had brought him back to himself, how he was a counselor now, helping other pastors work through moral failure in the ministry. He seemed like a new man and wanted me to know how much my father had meant to him. As Steve walked away my thoughts turned from death to resurrection. My heart felt light, playful to be honest. I was reminded again that because the God of new creation is at work everywhere around me, death is never the last word. *Baraka* missions always end in life.

What does all this mean for my calling and balance in life? God wants to turn me from a frustrated worker into a fearless kingdom player. Only a faith that listens to the promise of the EDEN project of God, that leaves the Babel mentality behind and that cleaves to God despite the challenges can really be used by him. God takes Abraham's small victories throughout his life and turns them into major triumphs in his mission. Today Abraham is celebrated as the head of the world's three monotheistic religions. Babel is forgotten except as a warning against personal and national self-reliance and God defiance. Those who do not believe in the mission of God are irrelevant to the future. Those who accept his call to leave folly's broken mission and playfully partner with God in all things are the ones God uses to bring *baraka* to his world.

Where does this kind of Abrahamic faith come from? It does not come from moralistic therapeutic deism. It only comes through encountering the God of Abraham. And we encounter God by practicing the disciplines that build belief. We accept God's mission by reading God's Word. We avoid self-reliance by cultivating a life of prayer and worship. We play for his mission by holding on to him in the ups and downs of life until we reach that place of playful shalom, happy to do his will because we are secure in his loving arms. Whatever our specific job and role in life, these disciplines of belief are necessary to becoming a kingdom player. God then takes our loaves and fish of daily work and worship and turns them into something of eternal consequence. He takes our little acts of loving and believing play and transforms them into something that changes the world.

When we believe like Abraham all our work, play and love become so many loaves and fish transformed into the building blocks of Eden regained

Thinking It Through

1. *Baraka* is defined as that which makes all things new and fully alive. As you look at Genesis 12:1-3, what are some specific areas that God was going to make alive? What additional dimensions of *baraka* does God add in the New Testament? (Think of a chapter like Romans 8.)

2. This chapter defines believing in God's mission as accepting his new mission, leaving folly's old mission and playing for God's mission even in the face of death. Which of these three elements of faith do you feel is strongest in your

life right now? Which element is weakest? Give reasons for your answer.

3. Playful work requires a sense of security and safety. What specific fears are keeping you from feeling God's strong powers in your life? What can be done to drive those fears away?

4. The call of Abraham means making a clear distinction between Babel projects of self-reliance and self-glory and *baraka* projects of playful delight. Babel projects lead to burnout; *baraka* projects lead to human flourishing. List some of your current projects in the areas of work, play and love. What elements of the Babel mentality can you detect? What would it take to shift to a *baraka* mentality? Pray daily for this shift for a solid week and then do your audit one more time. What changes can you see?

Taking Action

1. A good place to begin understanding the mission of God is the Gospel of Luke. Read through this book and examine each chapter for what it says about the mission of God, the God of mission and our place in that mission.

2. Play your pomodoro game today (see chapter 2). As you do each of the items on your to-do list, think of them as loaves and fish that you can offer up to the God of mission to use in his new creation. What new significance does this perspective give to your daily play?

chapter six

The Exodus Call to Freedom

The Cry for Freedom

The strongest call in the modern world may be the cry for freedom. Whether it is an Arab Spring, the democratization of the Global South or the overthrow of the latest taboo, freedom seems to be on everyone's mind. *Liberation* is a magic word, full of dreams about freedom from some external force, whether it be a bad job, a toxic family, a repressive church or society, the weight of tradition, oppressive child labor or dark supernatural forces that curse daily life. There is, however, a dark side to freedom. There is a voice inside of freedom that not only pushes us forward into the future but can push us over the cliff of ruin.

One of the current debates in American society is over what journalist Tom Wolfe called America's fifth freedom.[1] Wolfe noted that during World War II President Franklin Roosevelt rallied the nation by recalling four foundational freedoms of our great experiment. First was freedom from want. We believe in free markets because we believe that is the path to the greatest economic freedom and prosperity for the largest number of people. Second was freedom from fear. This meant a strong military that would secure our borders and defend our freedoms from external threats. Third was freedom of speech, where the lowliest citizen could speak his or her mind and not be punished. Finally, there was freedom of worship. In many ways this was the most fundamental freedom of all because it was what Roger Williams, the free-thinking Puritan founder

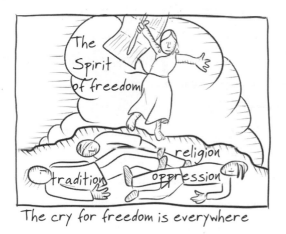

The cry for freedom is everywhere

of Rhode Island, had called soul freedom. This last freedom was the freedom of conscience. In many ways, it created the possibility of all the other freedoms. One trait that characterized these four freedoms was sustainability. Nothing inherent in the pursuit of prosperity, security, self-expression and worship could undermine these freedoms. This kind of freedom could last. Or so we thought.

In the 1960s, argues Wolfe, a youth revival created a fifth freedom: the freedom to do whatever we wanted without restrictions from religion or morality. In the land of the free, this was the only freedom left to try. It was an absolute freedom that was celebrated in movies, music and hedonistic lifestyles across the West and then across the world. It was fun. It was new. Wolfe ended his analysis by noting that the experiment in fifth freedom living was underway and we were all watching excitedly to see what would happen.

Here is what happened. America's fifth freedom began to endanger all the other freedoms. Free markets were shaken by the reckless and unchecked greed of Wall Street. Millions saw their savings and pensions dissolve in the worst financial crisis since the Depression. Speech was curbed by the cult of political correctness, in which only new ideas authorized by the fifth freedom mentality were allowed to be spoken in the public square. Terrorism without and mass shootings within broke the illusion of security. If the fifth freedom was taken seriously and anyone could do anything they wanted, then why not blow up my enemies or go on a killing spree to vent my anger and frustration with life? Worship changed as well. Christianity was under attack by a fifth freedom secularism that objected to its constraints on sexual experimentation, its narrow definitions of marriage and family, and right wing voting. Freedom entered the twenty-first century in a precarious position. It seems that real freedom cannot exist for long in a world where the fifth freedom runs riot.

The four freedoms defined American involvment in World War II

America added a 5th freedom in the 1960s, freedom to do whatever you want, and it put all the other freedoms at risk

Os Guinness, in his book *A Free People's Suicide*, offers a way forward.[2] The way to stabilize modern societies is not to take freedom away but to work together toward the renewal of sustainable freedom. Sustainable freedom, he argues, is based on a golden triangle created by America's founders, the architects of two of the greatest documents of human freedom in modern times, the Constitution (with its Bill of Rights) and the Declaration of Independence. The golden triangle of sustainable freedom is an interlocking trio of three central

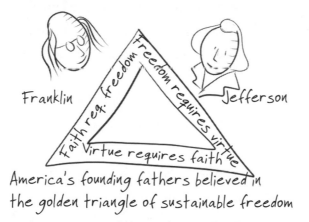

America's founding fathers believed in the golden triangle of sustainable freedom

values. First is the conviction that freedom cannot last without virtue or character. Free societies need moral people to sustain freedom. Second, virtue cannot last without faith. People may behave morally for a season, but without a strong conviction that virtue comes from a Creator who both sustains and judges all things, virtue becomes ephemeral. Finally, real faith cannot last without freedom. When faith is dictated or legislated it becomes false faith, worn as a veneer, not one that springs from the heart and animates all of life.

What does this discussion of sustainable freedom mean for our life balance and calling? What does it mean for emerging adults seeking great work, great play and great love? The Exodus call to freedom addresses these questions. It responds to the growing ideology of a fifth freedom world by offering a sustainable freedom that can flourish and grow indefinitely. Many Americans struggle with the fifth freedom mentality. They care about freedom in society and the rights of others. At the same time, they feel their freedom being threatened by a strange source: themselves. They detect impulses and areas of their life that are out of control.

For some, play is the area that is out of control. Many emerging adults feel that their hedonism is controlling them rather than the other way around. It is a fifth freedom that seems to be endangering all that the other freedoms cherish. Others worry as much about internal threats to freedom as the external ones. Fear and anger nip at my heels daily. What good is it if I have tons of external freedom when my slavery to negative emotions threatens to take this freedom away? So what if I live in a country that has a bill of rights and a free market economy. So what if the stories in my economy are full of more things to buy than I can number. What worries me most is this inner tyrant of anger or narcissism that threatens my personal world of work, play and love.

How can I be free inside and outside in a way that will last? The Exodus call in Exodus 19–20 shows the way toward a sustainable freedom in work, play and love, the key to being relevant to the mission of God in this world and balanced in all we do. Let's take a closer look.

The Exodus Call to Freedom

The children of Abraham had been called by God to liberate the world from the clutches of folly and her curse. Four hundred years into this amazing experiment,

Abraham's army of liberators end up as slaves of imperial Egypt. In their misery and despair, they cry out for the God of mission to arise and bring them back into the freedom of the mission of God. They want to return to their Abrahamic partnership with his *baraka* project of making all things new. God hears and acts.

Perhaps you have either read the story or seen the movies that recount the rise of Prince Moses, the plagues that broke Pharaoh's evil grip and the liberating exodus that led a million people out of bondage toward new life in a Promised Land. Heavy stuff, and arguably the most important event in the Old Testament.

Trouble, however, breaks out along the way. Some of it is external. They encounter hardships and dangers. But the greatest threat to their new freedom is not the armies of Pharaoh or the deprivations of the desert. The greatest threat is inside. The people think like slaves, feel like slaves and behave like slaves. They may have responded to the Exodus call of God but they are still listening to the call of folly, who keeps telling them to go back to bondage in Egypt where they would at least have enough to eat.

Exodus 19–20 (and 32) recount three actions of God to bring about sustainable internal and external freedom in his people and to silence the voice of folly.

First, he reminds them of their sacred story of freedom and calls them to live as free people before the watching world. In Exodus 19 we read these words:

> Then Moses went up to God, and the LORD called to him from the mountain and said, "This is what you are to say to the descendants of Jacob and what you are to tell the people of Israel: 'You yourselves have seen what I did to Egypt, and how I carried you on eagles' wings and brought you to myself. Now if you obey me fully and keep my covenant, then out of all nations you will be my treasured possession. Although the whole earth is

mine, you will be for me a kingdom of priests and a holy nation.' These are the words you are to speak to the Israelites." (vv. 3-6)

In Exodus 20:2 God reminds them of this foundational freedom found in the mission of God. "I am the LORD your God, who brought you out of Egypt, out of the land of slavery." Before freedom can be sustained, it has to be won. God not only calls us to freedom but won our freedom by his heroic acts of deliverance. And remembering that big win is a key part of sustaining freedom. The stories we tell ourselves over and over either strengthen or weaken our freedom. No people can remain free without memory. African countries that became free of colonial overlords in the sixties try hard to keep the memory of independence alive. In America the revolution of 1776 continues to be celebrated in a steady stream of books and media. Freedom needs a story.

Second, God gives the Israelites a constitution that will help them sustain freedom. These "laws" are not a contradiction of their freedom but instead the very conditions necessary for freedom to flourish, in the same way that the Bill of Rights reinforces our freedom and prevents others from taking it away. The laws create boundaries for

Freedom may be won through the barrel of a gun but it is best sustained through just laws

freedom and help protect me from not only the folly of others but also my own folly.

There are many ways to analyze the Ten Commandments. But what does a wisdom approach have to say? How do the Ten Commandments help us to follow the call of life in Proverbs 8? The call of Exodus 20 is a call to work, play and love with the triple delight that wisdom commends. When we keep our life free from idols, we are able to delight in the power and care of an almighty, missional God (commands 1-3), the condition of fearlessness that makes kingdom play possible. The last six commands call us to freedom in our relationships with others. They show us a way to be free from contempt for others and to delight in those we do his mission with and for. The fourth commandment on sabbath rest focuses on freedom in the area of identity. My true identity cannot be found in work or even in love. I am a much-loved child of the great King who has called me to playful delight in all of life. I am not a slave, either for Pharaoh or for God. Freedom from a slave mentality enables us to live lives of prayerful play.

Delighting in the God of Mission

The first three commandments deal with creating freedom from the idols that oppress.

"I am the LORD your God, who brought you out of Egypt, out of the land of slavery.

"You shall have no other gods before me.

"You shall not make for yourself an image in the form of anything in heaven above or on the earth beneath or in the waters below. You shall not bow down to them or worship them; for I, the LORD your God, am a jealous God, punishing the children for the sin of the parents to the third and fourth generation of those who hate me, but showing love to a thousand generations of those who love me and keep my commandments.

"You shall not misuse the name of the LORD your God, for the LORD will not hold anyone guiltless who misuses his name." (Exodus 20:2-7)

Genesis 12 reminds me that God's mission includes the restoration of delight. Restoring Eden means restoring God's place in human hearts and minds. Folly must be left behind if we would live in freedom. The gods of Egypt instilled only fear and oppression. The Egyptians, fearing those gods, treated the sons of Abraham like dirt. That experience of enslavement in Egypt, an enslavement done in the names of those gods, instilled a deep and debilitating fear in the power of those idols.

The way to break the bondage to an idol, whether mental or material, is not by having no gods but by having the true God—the God of creation, of Abraham, of liberating mission—as one's supreme delight and devotion. The exodus story is about the true and living God liberating enslaved people. If they go back to

The first three commands are about freedom from idols. Freedom means making the God of mission our only God.

their old gods they will also be going back to their old slavery. Worshiping the wrong gods leads to freedom lost. Freedom from gods that fail and frustrate comes through making the God of mission our only God.

Delighting in the Mission of God

The final six commands show us the way to sustainable freedom in level-two delight—delighting in whomever we work, love and play with and for.

> "Honor your father and your mother, so that you may live long in the land the LORD your God is giving you.
>
> "You shall not murder.
>
> "You shall not commit adultery.
>
> "You shall not steal.
>
> "You shall not give false testimony against your neighbor.
>
> "You shall not covet your neighbor's house. You shall not covet your neighbor's wife, or his male or female servant, his ox or donkey, or anything that belongs to your neighbor." (Exodus 20:12-17)

The command to honor our father and mother frees us from a contempt and resentment of authority and frees us to a life of treasuring and honoring family. The command to not murder calls us to more than just nonviolence. As Luther explains in his *Small Catechism*: "We should fear and love God that we may not hurt nor harm our neighbor in his body, but help and befriend him in every bodily need."[3] The deadly thoughts of rage that are part of the broken call are to be replaced by a delight in others that turns anger into godly sorrow, fear into love and bitterness into hope.

The command against adultery reminds us that we must not give away the freedom of lasting love by giving ourselves over to casual sex. The command to not steal reminds us that our purpose as God's missional children is to live not like orphans on the street but as princes in the palace. God provides for us as we partner with him in the royal mission. He takes care of our needs so that we can be free from the anxiety that would lead us to grab and seize. The command to not lie is a call to love our neighbor with our words. The tongue can kill, James reminds us, so we must live as free sons and daughters by speaking truth in love to our neighbors and about our neighbors.

Once we delight in the true and living God we are then free to love the other. The last six commands show us how to delight in whomever we work, play, love with and for.

The final command reminds us that level-two delight means freedom from envy. We cannot view our own lives and relationships with such discontent that we would throw them away and seek to steal another's. Rather than always longing to be doing something I'm not or possessing something I don't have (folly's approach to life and work) I learn to delight in what I have, in what I am doing now and in those I love.

Delighting in Whatever I Do Because of Who I Am and What I Am Becoming in Him

I have skipped the fourth commandment. What does it mean to remember the sabbath and keep it holy? Abraham Heschel, in his classic statement of Jewish spirituality, *The Sabbath*, declares that not only is the fourth command unique from all the others, but it is regarded by many Jewish commentators as the most important commandment of all.[4]

Eugene Peterson believes that the sabbath is a call to both pray and play.[5] He bases this on the two key Mosaic texts on the sabbath. The first, of course, is Exodus 20, which teaches that the purpose of the sabbath is to worship God and learn to depend on him. This sabbath rest is an island of prayer in a world and lifestyle with no time for God.

The second text, Deuteronomy 5:15, gives a different reason for the fourth command: "Remember that you were slaves in Egypt and that the LORD your God brought you out of there with a mighty hand and an outstretched arm. Therefore the LORD your God has commanded you to observe the Sabbath day." Because Israel lived in a land of bondage, where there was only work and no play, God gives them an island of play in a sea of busyness. Praying and playing, or prayerful play and playful prayer, are the heart of the sabbath and the essence of the fourth command.

What does that mean for our freedom? From this island of play and prayer I see the world around me differently. The first three commands remind me life is a battleground. There are idols to fight, sin to resist, demons to deal with. The last six commands remind me life is a village. There are people to care for, parents to honor, friends to be faithful to, lovers to treasure, property to protect for others. Both the spiritual warfare and the earthly care can be done either as Babel projects of self-reliance, self-glory and God-defiance or as *baraka* projects of fearless believing and playful cleaving to God's promises. Only the fourth commandment takes me out of the battlefield where I fight and out of the village where I serve, out to the island where I play with God. That is prayer. And then I play with his world. That is recreation. From this island, arms over-loaded with the exotic fruits of prayerful play and playful prayer, I return to the battleground and the village, animated by the nectar of God. I feast on the fruit of sabbath rest and engage in the prayerful play of village service. I drink the wine of sabbath rest and I engage in playful work of spiritual warfare.

How does this make me free? While the first three commands free me from fearful worship and to a liberated love for God, and the last six free me from servile work and to a liberated love for others, the fourth commandment liberates my self-image and identity. Even when I am freely fighting for the delight

The 4th command calls me to the sabbath
island of play and prayer where I am
loved not for what I do but simply for being
a child of God

of ever-loving arms and eyes or freely caring for others, I am still defined by what I do. Only on the island of play and prayer do I experience the deepest of all freedoms—being loved for who I am. I am valued simply for being God's child. The sabbath reminds me that the mission of God is never the basis of my partnership, only the result. The unconditional love and the unbreakable union of a parent with his child precede the work of war and the duties of caregiving. I must start each day on this island of grace and play and must return each evening to heal and be filled again with the freedom that only a child of the great king can enjoy. Armed with my fill of freedom from fear (the level-three delight of the wherever), I return to the mainland and engage in the playful work of worship and love. By living my life from an island base of prayer and play, I not only flourish in the work today, but I bear witness to the age to come, where the island and the mainland will merge forever in the new city of God.

A Champion of Freedom

I'd like to say that the children of Israel were transformed instantly into playful workers of the kingdom, free from the enslaving idols, identity and values of Egypt. I'd like to say that in their desert journeys and in their war for the Promised Land, they found that secret island and its exotic fruits of play and prayer. But that didn't happen. They needed a greater force to help them to sustain the freedom of the exodus event. They needed a champion.

Moses becomes that champion. The Israelites had been given their new constitution. God had shown them the path of freedom from their slave experience and slave mentality. But fear triumphed over faith. They forgot about the liberation from Egypt and went back to idols. They created a golden calf and gladly exchanged their delight in God's care and power for something much more limited that they could see and touch. Four hundred years earlier God had told Abraham that his *baraka* mission meant that he would curse any who attacked his people. So when his people betrayed one another, God brought internal judgment. He told Moses that he would turn against this people who had rejected him and his mission and create a new people of God who would be faithful to the Abraham call to mission.

Moses intervenes in Exodus 32:

> But Moses sought the favor of the Lord his God. "Lord," he said, "why should your anger burn against your people, whom you brought out of Egypt with great power and a mighty hand? Why should the Egyptians say, 'It was with evil intent that he brought them out, to kill them in the mountains and to wipe them off the face of the earth'? Turn from your fierce anger; relent and do not bring disaster on your people. Remember your servants Abraham, Isaac and Israel, to whom you swore by your own self: 'I will make your descendants as numerous as the stars in the sky and I will give your descendants all this land I promised them, and it will be their inheritance forever.'" Then the Lord relented and did not bring on his people the disaster he had threatened. (vv. 11-14)

We are all caught up in the war between wisdom and folly. We fight against folly's birth and the legacy of sin and sorrow that begins in the garden. We fight against her box of horrors and addictions. We fight to believe like Abraham and to experience the full freedom of the exodus and its call to liberating life. But our fight is doomed without a champion who will fight for us. Moses reminds us that freedom is never won in a single stroke. Sustainable freedom must be won again and again. The great champions who won our freedom in the past are gone, and we need others who can sustain that freedom for the present and the future.

In the moment that Moses stands between God and his righteous judgment and a people of mission who are refusing their call, the messianic dream is born. The rest of the Old Testament witnesses a growing hope for a champion who will sustain our freedoms, destroy our folly and restore our Eden. This champion is identified in the Gospels as Jesus the Messiah. We cannot simply read Exodus and pretend that we, unlike the generation of Moses, will sustain freedom and not fall back into folly and its lies. We need someone to fight for us, someone with whom we can partner to make sure that our work, play and love are full of playful delight that pleases God and satisfies us. We must not look at the law of freedom as achievable apart from a radical intervention by a powerful champion greater than ourselves. If freedom becomes just one more Babel project done in the spirit of self-reliance, self-glory and God-defiance, then it is freedom no longer.

Law of   Champion   Spirit
freedom   of freedom   of freedom

Sustainable Freedom

Freedom means more than simply
knowing the laws of freedom. We need
a champion of freedom who will fight for us
and give us the power to stay free.

When I live by these laws of freedom, I experience a new level of liberation. I have freedom to playfully delight in work, play and love. I have a new freedom to experience feelings of *fiero* and flow. Answering the Exodus calls means working out of a passion for the supremacy of my liberating God, out of love for my circle of relationships and out of a primary play that defines itself not by performance but by its childlike delight in God's "wherever work" as he builds his new creation all around me. This is sustainable freedom, and it is the greatest freedom of them all.

Thinking It Through

1. This chapter argues that the original Ten Commandments provide a structure for sustained freedom. From a gaming perspective, the only kind of freedom that can exist in a game is rule-based freedom—no rules, no game, no freedom. Can you think of examples in your own life where rules and standards made freedom possible?

2. Talk about fifth freedom culture. How do you see this fifth freedom approach to life affecting the world around you? How do you see it in advertising? TV programming? Your family members' lives? Work, school, church?

3. One of the key ideas in this chapter is that sabbath is an invitation to pray and play. It is the spirit of stress-free living and prayerful play, which then can renew all other areas of work and love. List some common objections to this view of the sabbath. How would you answer those objections in light of Proverbs 8 and the cluster of callings examined thus far?

Taking Action

1. Practice going through an entire day of "island" communication with the Spirit of God helping you pray. Focus on the Ten Commandments in your prayers. Pray that the freedom of delight in God, others and the liberated self of command four will set you free from bondage to idols and to slavish fear in your relationships.

2. Plan a half-day retreat. Your main purpose is to live on the island of rest and renewal for a few hours. This means becoming single-minded—seeing your overall purpose in life as delighting in being a much-loved child of God and gladly joining the family business by playing for the kingdom in all of life. Read through the Gospel of Matthew as your spiritual guide, and journal about how the example and teachings of Christ strengthen this single-minded focus on playing for the kingdom.

chapter seven

The David Call to Relationships

Networking or Village Building?

He was just the kind of CEO the board was looking for. Smart, charming, accomplished. His first few months at the helm of the promising new technology company were bright with promise. Then the rumors began: affairs with women in the office; a drinking problem; a power struggle with the board, shareholders and his team; misuse of funds. Then the resignation and the blame game. All of this followed by the search for the next new wonderworker to help the business achieve its dreams.

It's a story all too common. The new hire looks great on paper, is charming in the interview. But once the job starts and stress begins to build, he or she turns from Luke Skywalker to Darth Vader. When businesses hire, they always ask the competence question: Is he or she qualified to do the job? But increasingly human resource departments are asking about two other *C*s: What is the *character* of the candidate, and how will they contribute to positive *chemistry* in the company?

Relational skills—being trustworthy and respectful of others, honest and others-oriented—are becoming more and more important in corporate culture.

Motivational writers Stephen Covey and Jennifer Colosimo agree. They call for moving beyond networking, in which our contact with others is purely utilitarian, to "building a village." "Too often," they write, "networking comes down to having a lot of contacts on your iPhone or Blackberry. . . . Industrial Age thinking sees people as tools . . . as a 'means to an end.'" In networking, people "seek out others only when we need them, as we might go to a tool box for a

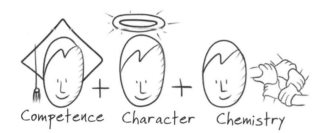

Competence   Character   Chemistry

In addition to competence, character and relational skills are becoming more important in corporate culture

	Industrial-Age Networking	Knowledge-Age Village Building
	Other people are a means to an end	Other people are important to me in and of themselves
	I seek people out when I need something from them	I seek people out to strengthen my relationship with them
	I have a large network of contacts	I belong to a village whose members care for one another

Networking vs. Village Building

hammer or a pair of scissors when you need it." Building a village, on the other hand, means caring for people. "The best networkers are building a village of people who value one another for more than what they can do for one another."[1] Their chart outlines the difference between traditional networking and the new emphasis on village building.

However, building a village is not something we can do at work and then ignore at home, church or play. Authenticity requires that we become people committed to village building in all these areas all the time.

How does this strategy of building a village connect with wisdom's call to the triple delight of the whatever, whomever and forever? We have heard the call of Eden to delight in whatever we do with playful work. We have heard Abraham's call to believe that we are part of the mission of God and to delight that he is working all around us making everything new. The call of Exodus encourages us to do all these things freely, to develop the sabbath habit of prayerful play as the heart of life.

What about the call to love? This is the focus of the present chapter and the following one. David's call will teach us a very important feature of building our village: learning to fight for delight in our circle of influence.

David, King of Hearts: Fighting for Delight in His Circle of Influence

David's life, from his anointing as king in his youth to his ascent to the united throne of Israel decades later, is a story of passion, intrigue, danger, betrayal and intense relationships. Through it all, his winding path to power is marked by consistent village building. The primary skill he displays and develops in this period of his life is fighting for delight in God and God's people when attacked by external enemies.

He sings about this delight in some of the earliest psalms. About his people he sings, "I say of the holy people who are in the land, 'They are the noble ones in whom is all my delight'" (Psalm 16:3). Connected to this delight in God's people is his delight in the God of his people. In Psalm 37:4 he sings about "[delighting] in the LORD, and he will give you the desires of your heart."

This fight for double delight marked his lifestyle and his leadership style in the first phase of his career. Consider the story of David's battle against Goliath. For many of us, this is a story about never giving up, even against long odds, about the little guy beating the giant. The biblical historian who recorded David's life and reign saw it a little differently.

Fighting & Delighting

David's call is to fight for delight in our village of relationships

First Samuel 17 reveals David's early attitudes about the fight for delight and how God uses it in his mission to save the world. Young David arrives on the battlefield to deliver food to his ungrateful brothers and learns of the Philistine giant whose challenge to personal combat has been met with a cowardly silence by the entire army of Israel, including their king, Saul. David burns with indignation over this state of affairs. He is ashamed of his people and of his king. David is also concerned about the fear he sees paralyzing the people he loves. This fear threatens the mission of Israel as a light to the nations and the *baraka* project of healing the nations. But rather than descending into contempt and complaint, he makes a bold move: "David said to Saul, 'Let no one lose heart on account of this Philistine; your servant will go and fight him'" (1 Samuel 17:32). He decides to fight for the delight of God's people and to restore his own delight in the army of God.

But he fights not just for delight in his people; he fights to delight in God as well. The shadow of imminent defeat at the hand of the Philistines threatens their delight in God as much as their mission for God: "Where were you, God, when Goliath paralyzed our troops in fear? Where were you when the Philistines overran us on the field of battle and defeated us and, by implication, your mission?" David heads out to face Goliath, confident in God's loving eyes and arms, and declares his purpose in facing down this intimidating enemy. David's defiant words are captured in 1 Samuel 17:46: "This day the LORD will deliver you into my hands, and I'll strike you down and cut off your head. This very day I will give the carcasses of the Philistine army to the birds and the wild animals, and the whole world will know that there is a God in Israel." With the cry, "The battle is the Lord's," he attacks his nine-foot challenger, felling him with a single

David & Goliath is about fighting for delight
in the God of mission & in the mission of God

stone and precipitating the rout of Israel's enemies. Delight in God's people is restored. Delight in God is restored as well.

David's heroics on the field of battle win him the adulation of the people and the hatred of the king. Saul eventually plots to destroy David to remove this threat to his throne, so David and a few loyal followers are forced to flee into the wilderness, where they are hunted like wild beasts. Where is his village of relationships now? Where is the God he delights in? Where are the people that had cheered him on a few years earlier? Through all those years of dodging his hunters and being exiled from his own nation, David never gives up the fight for delight. Instead he relies on playful prayer to turn his disillusionment into delight. Psalm 42:10-11 is typical of the way David handles the enmity of the world and the apparent abandonment by his God:

> *My bones suffer mortal agony*
> *as my foes taunt me,*
> *saying to me all day long,*
> *"Where is your God?"*
> *Why, my soul, are you downcast?*
> *Why so disturbed within me?*
> *Put your hope in God,*
> *for I will yet praise him,*
> *my Savior and my God.*

Throughout this period David is able to show love for his great enemy Saul. He refused to harm him in any way even though he had ample opportunity. David loved Saul's son Jonathan even though King Saul was against him. He loved his sworn enemy Achish, king of the Philistines, who in turn loved him like a son after David sought refuge in the enemy kingdom. He fought for his marriage to Saul's daughter Michel. He fought for his second wife, Abigail. He delighted in his fighting men and earned their lifelong trust. Despite terrible circumstances around him, he continued to build a village, fighting for delight in God and others against all odds. He never gave up on God or people. At least at first.

David, King of Fools: Failing in the Fight for Delight

Eventually David learns what happens to our circle of influence when we stop fighting for delight. David stops fighting for delight in God and the people God has given him beginning with the Bathsheba scandal. The story tells us that one day from the roof of his palace he spotted a beautiful woman bathing. He should have been out fighting with his men but instead he is lazy and distracted in the palace. Against every impulse of common sense, David listened to the voice of folly and started a deadly affair. Not only did he commit adultery, but he also arranged the killing of an innocent man, Bathsheba's husband, Uriah. Shortly after, his world came crashing down. He watched the baby born to Bathsheba die. He was confronted and condemned by Nathan the prophet. Seeds of permanent discord were sown in his kingdom. His village breaks.

Why did David let this happen? Second Samuel 12:8-9 gives us three clues to his destructive behavior. The Lord speaks through Nathan the prophet: "I gave your master's house to you, and your master's wives into your arms. I gave you all Israel and Judah. *And if all this had been too little, I would have given you even more.* Why did you *despise* the word of the LORD by doing what is evil in his eyes?" (emphasis added). David had stopped fighting for delight in his circle of influence and replaced it instead with a threefold despising. He despised the relationships God had given him, the word of God and the heart of God to give him even more if he had but trusted him.

David quit fighting for delight in his village when he allowed contempt for his whatever, whomever and wherever to control his life

Despising is more about contempt than hate. To despise is to look down on something or someone as worthless. The heart that despises looks at its village and says, "I deserve more, I need more." The habit of despising leads to envy and entitlement: "I have nothing to be grateful for because I have been given nothing worthy of me. All my blessings are insults to my self-image." When I am discontent with whatever I am doing, whomever I am doing it with and with the infinite security and love that surrounds me, I am replacing delight with despising.

When we no longer delight in our circle of belonging we can no longer love or lead others in our village effectively. David struggled as a leader during those years of despising and almost saw his entire kingdom collapse, beginning with his daughter, Tamar. She was brutally raped by her brother Amnon, and David did nothing about it. He didn't fight for delight in his family, and failed to restore righteousness and love where there was abuse and violation.

He didn't fight for delight in Absalom, his outraged son, driven mad with rage by the rape of his sister. Absalom consequently rejected the failed leadership of his father and tried to seize power. Only too late, after his son's death, did David's tears speak of his love for Absalom.

There was more war, the Sheba rebellion, the rebellion of Adonijah, another son. Again and again David seemed unable to summon his fighting spirit. Only after Bathsheba fought for her son Solomon's right of succession did David rise to become the relational leader he once was.

What do we make of David, king of fools? We might say that these events were not his fault; David just had bad luck or faced the judgment of God. But we would miss an important point. When we stop fighting for delight in our circle of influence, the circle falls apart. That is what happened to David. There is tragedy in this great leader's failure. When one stops the fight for delight one stops building the village God wants. Like Shakespeare's King Lear, David's apathy led to war, rebellion and near ruin for the people entrusted to his care.

Some years ago I read a story in the news titled "Together in Poverty, Apart in Riches"[2] that told of a couple who had fought for delight in one another during the hard years of trying to build a family and a business. Once they were successful and comfortable, however, the marriage started falling apart. The causes of this collapse? The usual suspects. Contempt. Lack of appreciation. Love of money. Their marriage seemed small and insignificant in light of the power and prosperity they now enjoyed. Despising replaced delighting, and they broke apart.

This story could happen to any of us. Once we stop the fight for delight, contempt and despising take over, raid our village and burn it to the ground.

David, Child of the King: Restoring Delight

Thankfully, David's relational failures are the not the end of the story. Early in his life David had learned two important skills of the relational leader. As a young man he had learned about the fighting spirit as he fought for people and not against them. As a young king he had learned the importance of the spirit of delight. He had treasured his people, his family and his God as the most important things in life and had learned how to protect this treasure with praise of his great King and honor in his relationships with others.

With the triumph of folly in his life and the rise of contempt for God and others, David needed to learn two additional skills of village building: *turning around* and *trusting upward*. What is turning around? It means going back to treasuring God and the people in our lives after a period of turning away in contempt. It is the prodigal coming to his senses in the far country and walking the long road home. It is realizing one was wrong and doing something about it. We see David's turning in Psalm 51.

When we turn around, we admit that we have despised the treasures of God and others, and we come to our senses, valuing the precious lives in our village once again and taking up the good work of village building.

The final skill of village building is perhaps the most

> Have mercy on me, O God,
>   according to your unfailing love;
> according to your great compassion
>   blot out my transgressions. . . .
> Create in me a pure heart, O God,
>   and renew a steadfast spirit within me.
> Do not cast me from your presence
>   or take your Holy Spirit from me.
> Restore to me the joy of your salvation
>   and grant me a willing spirit, to sustain me.
> Then I will teach transgressors your ways,
>   so that sinners will turn back to you.
> **PSALM 51:1, 10-13**

important: learning to trust upward in the God of mission. David discovered that every relational leader in home, church or nation must learn to be useful to God and his world. He realized that he could fight and delight and repent effectively because God was fighting and delighting for him. The fight for delight wasn't all on his shoulders. God fights for us in our battle for delight.

David restores the fight for delight
by turning around and trusting up

Trusting upward was a lesson David should have learned earlier in his reign. In 2 Samuel 7, God called David to go beyond level one and two fighting and delighting to the level three delight of trusting in God's strong arms and the forever security and safety that he provides. This is called the Davidic covenant and it is all about trusting in a God who delights in us and our village and fights for it with all his might. Ultimately this covenant is about God providing the Messiah, but it had implications for how David playfully delighted in his circle of influence. Sadly, it took David a lifetime to understand these words from 2 Samuel 7:

I have been with you wherever you have gone, and I have cut off all your enemies from before you. Now I will make your name great, like the names of the greatest men on earth. And I will provide a place for my people Israel and will plant them so that they can have a home of their own and no longer be disturbed. Wicked people will not oppress them anymore, as they did at the beginning and have done ever since the time I appointed leaders over my people Israel. I will also give you rest from all your enemies.

The LORD declares to you that the LORD himself will establish a house for you: When your days are over and you rest with your ancestors, I will raise up your offspring to succeed you, your own flesh and blood, and I will establish his kingdom. . . . Your house and your kingdom will endure forever before me; your throne will be established forever. (vv. 9-12, 16)

During his time of despising and destroying, David neglected this promise of a God who fights for us and delights in us, a God who wants to build a house for us, to build our village for us and with us. But in his last moments, when he returned to his identity as a much-loved child of God, the beauty and wonder of this work of God came back to him. In his last words recorded in 2 Samuel 23:5, David cries out:

> *If my house were not right with God,*
> *surely he would not have made with me an*
> *everlasting covenant,*
> *arranged and secured in every part;*
> *surely he would not bring to fruition my salvation*
> *and grant me my every desire.*

What gives me freedom from worry and fear in the moment of crisis or threat? A God who fights for me, delights in me and will build my village even when I fail.

Covey and Colosimo are onto something in their preference for village building over conventional networking. The call of David is the call to be a king or queen of hearts, to fight for delight in our village of relationships. We have to be honest about our tendency to let folly fill us with contempt for our village. For life to flourish, for work, play and love to be rich and full, we need to heed

Even when we fail, the God of mission fights for delight in our village of relationships

the call of David. We need to learn how to fight and delight as well as how to turn around and trust upward. Only as we delight in the God of wherever will we be able to restore delight in the whatever and the whomever.

Thinking It Through

1. In 1 Samuel 17:46 David explains what drives his fight for delight in God and in God's people. Review this verse, and put David's motives into your own words.

2. David loses his fighting spirit and the playful delight in others that made him so relevant to the mission of God. The prophet Nathan confronts him in 2 Samuel 12:8-9 and accuses him of "taking things for granted." What examples most clearly reveal this attitude in David?

3. David's return to God-centered work, play and love involves trusting and turning. Read Psalm 51. What specific expressions of trusting and turning can you find in this psalm?

4. Reread 2 Samuel 7:9-12 and 23:5. What role did the Davidic covenant of 2 Samuel 7 play later in David's life to help restore him to that fighting spirit?

5. Draw a village map. Put yourself in the center and then draw spokes and circles from that center, indicating some of your key relationships. Add names to the circles. Which of the building skills (fighting for delight, turning from despising and contempt, trusting that God is fighting for your village) are you exercising in your village?

Taking Action

1. Read Psalm 73, written by the worship leader Asaph, an associate of David. Note his descent into contempt early in the psalm and the restoration of delight in God and life with God by the end. Write your own version of Psalm 73.

2. Identify a key relationship in which you need to fight for delight. Download some information from Peacemakers International on how to resolve interpersonal conflict. Read this material and then make a plan to bring about restoration and renewal.

3. One way to turn away from contempt and restore delight is to turn your contempt and anger into sorrow. *Cry of the Soul* by Tremper Longman and Dan Allender is a very useful guide to how to do this.[3] Consider studying this book and learning the art of turning hurt, anger and contempt into a godly and "sweet" sorrow that leads back to the path of delight.

chapter eight

The Singers' Call to Lovemaking

Kiss me full on the mouth" is a startling way to open a book, particularly a book of the Bible. Yet the Song of Songs (sometimes known as Song of Solomon) opens with this dramatic call to romantic love. As with the call of David, this call is part of the call to love, a crucial branch in our tree of life. However, before we look at this collection of songs and the call that it issues, we first need to talk about modern views of romantic love.

Love in Trouble

There is a growing consensus that the music of love in the modern world is horribly off key. Love, sexuality and committed relationships are all in trouble. One expression of the problem is the practice of hooking up. Over the past ten years, young people in their twenties have moved from a culture of dating, courtship and eventual commitment to a culture of casual sex as a way to delay commitment. Why let love and a high maintenance relationship get in the way of a career and further schooling? Better to meet your need for sex with relative strangers, thus avoiding unwanted entanglements. The modern call to relationships is simple: sex without love, at least for now.

Lena Dunham's award-winning HBO television show *Girls* depicts this hook-up culture. The likable singles in the show have lots of sex but little love. They hook up often, but it is typically awkward, degrading and depressing.

One reason for the rise of the hook-up culture is the delay of marriage until later in one's twenties. The US Census Bureau highlights this trend. In 1960 the average age of first marriage was just under twenty-three for men and just over twenty for women. By 2005 the average age had risen by nearly five years to twenty-seven for

Lena Dunham's "Girls":
lots of sex, very little love

men and twenty-five for women. Postponing marriage has meant more sexual activity with a variety of partners but seldom with a view to commitment.

Some feminists argue that this new approach is empowering and liberating for women, closing the gap of the old double standard that winked at male promiscuity but condemned women who exercised their sexual freedom. This reading

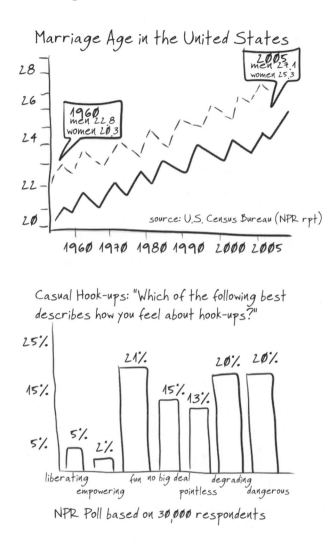

Marriage Age in the United States

source: U.S. Census Bureau (NPR rpt)

Casual Hook-ups: "Which of the following best describes how you feel about hook-ups?"

NPR Poll based on 30,000 respondents

may not fit the facts, however. A recent NPR poll numbering some thirty thousand respondents gives a more complex picture of hook-up culture. When asked the question "Which of the following [words] best describes how you feel about hookups?" only a very small percentage chose "liberating" and "empowering" (5% and 2% respectively). In contrast, a significantly higher percentage described hookups as "degrading" (20%), "dangerous" (20%) and "pointless" (13%).

Marriage Under Attack

Is marriage the answer to this crazy hook-up culture? Maybe, maybe not. Many emerging adults are rethinking marriage. Let's look at the modern critique of marriage through our fictional friend Mia.

Mia thinks a lot about marriage. Some days she dreams about finding the right guy and living happily ever after. In her heart of hearts, however, she has deep reservations about modern marriage. She looks at her parents' marriage and mentally recites the litany of horrors that she sees. Her father and mother seem to have little respect for each other. They complain about and criticize one another constantly. Aren't married couples supposed to be compatible? Her parents seem to have nothing in common. They constantly sin against each other. For example, they lie to each other about little things (spending, where they have been) and accuse each other falsely.

Mia's mother has shared more personal things with her daughter lately, things that have made Mia deeply uncomfortable. Her mother complained about her lack of satisfying intimacy with Mia's father. Mia's mother also revealed how exhausting they sometimes find one another's company. Instead of the home being a place of renewal and rest, it's more like a battleground where the tensions in the marriage drain away what little energy is left from the day. Added to this is the financial pressure of owning a home, the time pressures of trying to work on a marriage with all the other commitments of work and social life, and the stress of arguing with each other on an almost daily basis.

Mia is shaken by these conversations with her mother. She wonders whether marriage can deliver on her dreams. Mia needs to hear the call to multilevel lovemaking. She needs a new perspective on love and marriage. The singers just might have what she needs.

Is There a Better Way?

Two of the wisdom books of the Bible, Proverbs and Song of Songs, offer a different approach to love and sexuality than the ones envisioned by either Lena or Mia. The hook-up culture seems to be heeding the voice of folly with its urging to do whatever we feel like while disregarding the consequences. Traditional marriage seems equally unappealing, with its many miserable examples and high divorce rates. There is, however, a third way between traditional marriage and hooking up. Lady Wisdom issues an intriguing summons to what we might call multilevel lovemaking. Let's take a closer look. The call can be heard in its clearest form in Proverbs 5:18-21. Here is how *The Message* puts it:

> *Bless your fresh-flowing fountain!*
> *Enjoy the wife you married as a young man!*
> *Lovely as an angel, beautiful as a rose—*
> *don't ever quit taking delight in her body.*
> *Never take her love for granted!*
> *Why would you trade enduring intimacies for cheap*
> *thrills with a whore?*
> *for dalliance with a promiscuous stranger?*
> *Mark well that GOD doesn't miss a move you make;*
> *he's aware of every step you take.*

Proverbs 5 is an echo of Genesis 2:24 and the call to leave father and mother, cleave to one another and become one flesh. The leaving, cleaving and uniting process offers a picture of marriage as multilevel lovemaking with sexual love as but one expression of this complex and layered life together. It is important to remember, for example, that friendship love is the explicitly stated reason for marriage (although obviously not the only reason) because it was not good for man "to be alone" (Genesis 2:18).

What are the various levels of this marital lovemaking? The Greek language has four different words for love, which C. S. Lewis wrote about.[1] There is *eros*, sexual love. *Storge*, or natural affection, is the kind of love we have for family

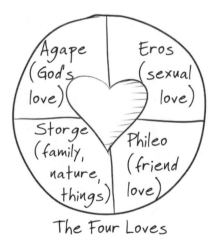

The Four Loves

members. *Phileo* is friendship love. And there is the favorite Christian term for love, *agape*, pointing to the source of all love and the unconditional, sacrificial love that comes from God.

The Song of Songs has been ascribed to Solomon, who knew a thing or two about romantic love (having had 1000 wives and concubines), but the reference to Solomon in 1:1 may refer to the book being either by Solomon or to Solomon (the Hebrew supports either translation).[2] Either way, Song of Songs encourages *eros* love in marriage but shows that this is done in the context of multilevel lovemaking. In the lyrics of the singers we hear a call to make love that is intensely erotic, committed to *phileo*, appreciative of *storge* and dependent on *agape*.

God's call to lovemaking is therefore a marriage that makes love on four levels. Committed lovers are to make *phileo* by building the respect and mutual sub-

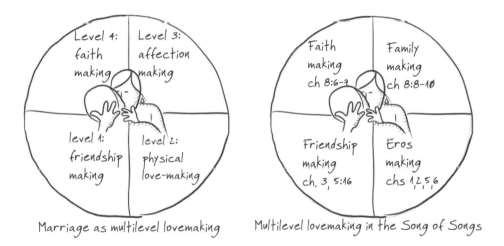

Marriage as multilevel lovemaking   Multilevel lovemaking in the Song of Songs

mission that is the heart of friendship; to make *eros* by sexual play and intercourse; to make *storge* by building families and connecting with their extended families; and to make *agape* through worship, spiritual disciplines, Christian community and partnership in God's mission.

First, the lovers make friendship love throughout the song. They seem to love spending time with each other, conversing with each other and doing things together. Even in their moments of passion they celebrate that they are simultaneously making friendship love. We hear this in 5:16:

> *His mouth is sweetness itself;*
> *he is altogether lovely.*
> *This is my beloved, this my friend,*
> *daughters of Jerusalem.*

Eros is there in all its intensity, but so is *phileo* with all of its companionship, acceptance and mutual respect.

Second, the singers make *eros* throughout the book. The language of their sexual passion is explicit, erotic and eloquent. They delight in one another's bodies without limit. They drink deeply at the well of romantic love. In chapter 4 the lovers stand before one another naked and amazed at the beauty of each other's body. The man declares,

> *Your breasts are like fawns,*
> *twins of a gazelle, grazing among the first spring flowers.*
> *The sweet, fragrant curves of your body,*
> *the soft, spiced contours of your flesh*
> *Invite me, and I come. I stay*
> *until dawn breathes its light and night slips away.*
> *You're beautiful from head to toe, my dear love,*
> *beautiful beyond compare, absolutely flawless.*
> **SONG OF SOLOMON 4:5-7 *THE MESSAGE***

The woman is equally direct in her ecstasy:

> *His arms are rods of gold*
> *set with topaz.*
> *His body is like polished ivory*
> *decorated with lapis lazuli.*
> **SONG OF SONGS 5:14**

Their *eros* lovemaking is full of delight, pleasure and intensity.

Third, the lovers frequently punctuate their *eros* lovemaking to express appreciative love for their families and the role the family plays in preparing lovers for their life together. They sing family's role in their love in 8:8-9:

> *We have a little sister,*
> *and her breasts are not yet grown.*
> *What shall we do for our sister*
> *on the day she is spoken for?*
> *If she is a wall,*
> *we will build towers of silver on her.*
> *If she is a door,*
> *we will enclose her with panels of cedar.*

This protective role of the family is crucial for the fullness of love. The lovers further express the value of *storge* in preparing them for the other levels of love. Note 2:7, which warns of not arousing *eros* until the right time. This is the role of *storge* lovemaking—to keep *eros* within the boundaries of marriage and family approval. Family love is not to be seen as a burdensome restriction but rather is to be appreciated for keeping *eros* safe for the lovers to enjoy forever.

Though the Song of Songs says little of God directly, the lovers sing in chapter 8 about *agape* lovemaking, the faith and trust in God to pour out his *agape* on the lovers and thereby conquer death, disaster, greed and the ravages of time.

> *Place me like a seal over your heart,*
>   *like a seal on your arm;*
> *for love is as strong as death,*
>   *its jealousy unyielding as the grave.*
> *It burns like blazing fire,*
>   *like a mighty flame.*
> *Many waters cannot quench love;*
>   *rivers cannot sweep it away.*
> *If one were to give*
>   *all the wealth of one's house for love,*
>   *it would be utterly scorned. (vv. 6-7)*

As they sing to each other these words of faith, they engage in *agape* lovemaking that lifts up human love into its highest realm and ultimate source. They have become fully alive lovers who live in the intense center of multilevel lovemaking.

Multilevel Lovemaking in Ephesians

The melody of the Song of Songs can be heard again in the New Testament. Paul rhapsodizes about fourfold lovemaking in the context of marriage in Ephesians 5. The key verse for multilevel lovemaking is 5:21, "Submit to one another out of reverence for Christ." This mutual submission is *phileo*—the love of friends. Friends see each other as equals and have no trouble sharing the circle of friendship with a third party ("out of reverence for Christ"). They practice the mutual give-and-take of good friends. Upon that foundation of friendship love the other loves can then be built.

In Ephesians 5:22 Paul calls on the woman to take the lead in this friendship love by initiating *phileo* in her marriage. Respect is the foundation for all friendship, and the mutual respect between best friends doesn't just happen; it has to be built. So too in marriage. Respect is crucial if the marriage is to be strong. The woman is asked to build the marriage by building *phileo*. There are clearly limits to what this "honoring" is to look like. She is called to show honor to the man in whatever ways are consistent with the respect she gives to Christ. This respect given to Christ as her head is also an expression of friendship love because Christ, though our master, also calls us friend (John 15:13-16). Even with Jesus, there can be no friendship without the honor and respect displayed by loving and free obedience (John 15:14). Paul expresses this *phileo* lovemaking as follows:

> Wives, submit yourselves to your own husbands as you do to the Lord. For the husband is the head of the wife as Christ is the head of the church, his body, of which he is the Savior. Now as the church submits to Christ, so also wives should submit to their husbands in everything. (Ephesians 5:22-24)

In Western cultures where friendships are based on common interests, humor and familiarity, this call to *phileo* lovemaking may seem strange, but in any culture there can be no lasting friendship without showing respect and honoring the other's wishes and will. Paul acknowledges the mutuality of this honoring of each other's will in 5:21.

Second, the husband is asked to take the initiative in *agape* lovemaking, pouring God's love, acceptance, grace and *baraka* into the life of his wife.

> Husbands, love your wives, just as Christ loved the church and gave himself up for her to make her holy, cleansing her by the washing with water through the word, and to present her to himself as a radiant church, without stain or wrinkle or any other blemish, but holy and blameless. (Ephesians 5:25-27)

The spiritual beauty that results from the *agape* lovemaking heightens the pleasures of *eros*.

Third, this love includes *storge* as the parents pour their love into their parents and children. Paul writes in Ephesians 6:1-4:

> Children, obey your parents in the Lord, for this is right. "Honor your father and mother"—which is the first commandment with a promise—"so that it may go well with you and that you may enjoy long life on the earth."
>
>   Fathers, do not exasperate your children; instead, bring them up in the training and instruction of the Lord.

The climax of this multilevel lovemaking comes in Ephesians 5:31 as erotic lovemaking intertwines their bodies in a union of ecstasy: "For this reason a man will leave his father and mother and be united to his wife, and the two will become one flesh."

Ephesians, at least indirectly, reflects Song of Songs and Proverbs 5 in calling for multilevel lovemaking. More clearly than either of those two Old Testament passages, however, it shows how much *eros* depends on *phileo*. Without friendship there can be no lasting *eros*. Fully alive lovers feel the full multilevel intensity of God's love in Christ in all of their lovemaking.

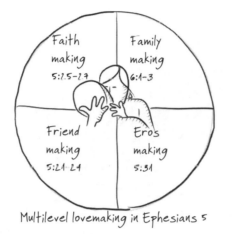

Multilevel lovemaking in Ephesians 5

Marriage, Lovemaking and Flow

Is this call to multilevel lovemaking too idealistic? What about Mia's parents? Their problems seem so many that a fourfold love seems out of reach. Or is it? The purpose of this rich and varied lovemaking is not simply to store up all kinds of wonderful love but to use it in fully engaging the problems in your marriage.

This is what flow is all about. Flow is that desirable state of being in which you feel fully alive by engaging a challenge that perfectly matches your resources. When we mobilize the love, grace, truth, *eros*, *agape*, *phileo* and *storge* at our disposal and fully employ them in meeting problems like those in Mia's parents' marriage (lack of respect, sinning against one another, sexual selfishness, etc.), then we can experience a state of flow. In other words, problems in a marriage are not the enemies of flow but the conditions for flow to be achieved. Make love on all four levels and then pour all of the love available into meeting the challenges. Watch flow turn negatives into positives. Great games and great highs are about overcoming great challenges.

Resources

Multilevel lovemaking generates the love needed for all the challenges

Challenges

Most deal with violations of love on the levels of friendship, family, sex or lack of grace and mercy

The challenges of marriage coupled with multilevel lovemaking create the conditions for flow

What About Singles?

In his book *The Meaning of Marriage,* Tim Keller writes that, in light of the mission of God, all relationships are about helping to prepare the other for the new creation.[3] What that means is that our relationships have a future orientation. They are opportunities to help friends, family members or a beloved long for the day when all things are fully alive and to begin to live for that day now. This involves discerning our calling and living out that calling in the world. That is what I have been attempting to address in this book.

For single people, God asks them to store up *eros* for the future marriage relationship he may have for them. But while they may be less active in *eros* lovemaking, they can be more active in *agape*, *phileo* and *storge* lovemaking because they have more time to give to these other levels of lovemaking. This means that the single person can not only live life full of love but also help others prepare for the new creation and empower others to participate now in the mission of God. Jesus and Paul are but two of the most important examples of the power of three-level lovemaking in partnering with the mission of God.

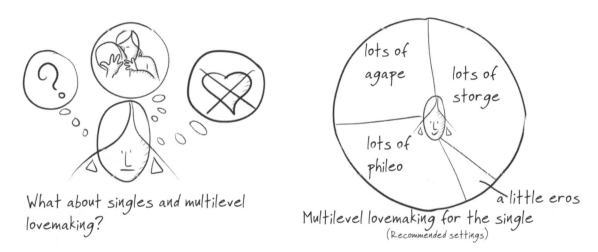

What about singles and multilevel lovemaking?

Multilevel lovemaking for the single
(Recommended settings)

For sexually active millennials the call to pull back on runaway *eros* so that the other loves can increase may be greeted with skepticism. But millennial singles should consider the benefit of such a strategy: love that is fully alive. One can go the route of loveless sex that is recreational at best and degrading at worst, or one can choose something more. That more only comes through following the path of wisdom and developing multilevel lovemaking from the beginning of young adulthood. As a relationship moves through the various stages of maturity with *storge, agape* and *phileo* growing stronger and stronger, then *eros* can grow as well. Now runaway *eros* becomes designer *eros*—*eros* as the Designer intended, weaving artfully with the other golden threads of multilevel lovemaking.

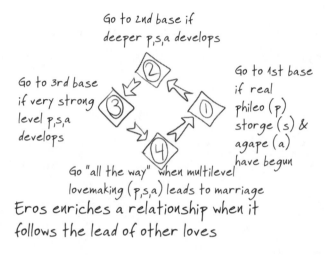

Go to 2nd base if deeper p,s,a develops

Go to 3rd base if very strong level p,s,a develops

Go to 1st base if real phileo (p) storge (s) & agape (a) have begun

Go "all the way" when multilevel lovemaking (p,s,a) leads to marriage

Eros enriches a relationship when it follows the lead of other loves

What About What Other People Think?

No matter what advice is given on the subject of sexual guidelines for singles, there will always be a range of opinions and reactions. Some will object that freedom is being restricted. Others will object that such thinking is too liberal and singles need to "just say no." Still others who are confused will simply follow the position that yells the loudest. God calls us to wisdom living, however, not just conservatism, liberalism or confusion. I have found Romans 14 helpful in finding the path of wisdom through the maze of conservative pharisees who say no to anything new, liberals who say yes to anything new, and the confused majority that sway from side to side. The basic principle of Romans 14 is to follow the way of love. Consider these verses:

> If your brother or sister is distressed because of what you eat, you are no longer acting in love. Do not by your eating destroy someone for whom Christ died. Therefore do not let what you know is good be spoken of as evil. For the kingdom of God is not a matter of eating and drinking, but of righteousness, peace and joy in the Holy Spirit, because anyone who serves Christ in this way is pleasing to God and receives human approval.
>
> Let us therefore make every effort to do what leads to peace and to mutual edification. (vv. 15-19)

There seem to be four models of decision making alluded to in these verses. First is the way of no. This refers to the Christian pharisee who seeks to dictate to everyone else. The passage above tells us to resist the condemning voice of the pharisee ("do not let what you know is good be spoken of as evil"). Second is the way of yes. This is the stronger brother who enjoys his freedom in Christ but may throw around his freedom so recklessly that it actually destroys other Christians ("do not by your eating destroy someone for whom Christ died"). The third decision-making model is the way of fear ("If your brother or sister is distressed because of what you eat"). It is that of the younger or weaker brother who is confused about what to do and will follow the loudest voice in the room at the risk of violating his own conscience. Just as we are unyielding to the pharisee so we must be sensitive and flexible to the weaker brother. The fourth model, and the one commended by Paul, is the way of love. This is the peacemaker model of verse 19 ("Let us therefore make every effort to do what leads to peace and to mutual edification").

Wise decision making resists the negativism of the pharisee and the reckless insensitivity of the stronger brother even while it seeks a unique path that will

way of no	way of fear	way of yes	way of love
The legalist	The weaker brother	The strong one	The mature brother
"My way is God's way"	"I don't know the way"	"Do whatever you want"	"Do whatever builds up" -don't abuse freedom -don't follow crowd -don't be bullied

Romans 14 and the 4 decision-making models

lead the younger brother to life. When we are trying to make wise decisions about sexual practice and love practice in the modern world we need to heed the way of wisdom and navigate effectively through the choices of easy noes, easy yeses or confusing fear.

So What?

So what does this call to multilevel lovemaking mean for my day-to-day life? Let me make four suggestions.

First, multilevel lovemaking for single and married people is a political act in a culture of God-defiance where self is the new tyrant. The flower children of the 1960s saw the political implications of sexuality when they uttered their famous anti-Vietnam slogan, "Make love, not war." When we do something so deeply countercultural as committing to love someone on all levels for all of life, we are shaking the system. We are acting politically. We are challenging the sovereignty of the self and showing our loyalties to the sovereign mission of God and the God of that mission. Don't trivialize sexuality and lovemaking. It is a public and powerful statement of the politics of the kingdom that is coming.

Second, multilevel lovemaking gives us new ways to rekindle delight with our spouse. Sex is not always about sex. Sexual issues may be rooted in one of the other levels. It may be about communication. It may be about money. It may be about sin, self-loathing, worship or lack of respect. Fixing a problem in the bedroom may mean spending more time in the game room, the living room or the prayer room.

In an age in which sex has become a commodity, making love is a political act

Wild eros devours all the other loves

Third, the call to multilevel lovemaking addresses the question "Why wait?" If eros is just about sex and having fun, then why wait? But what if you want to be a fully alive lover? If you have been called to real, fully alive lovemaking then do not arouse *eros* before it is time because *eros* will burn all the other loves down. It devours its friends. When you have sex with a friend, the friendship is never the same. When you push God away so you can do what you want with *eros, agape* evaporates. When you have to lie to your parents or a sibling to protect your stolen *eros, storge* takes a huge hit. You shrink as a multilevel lover when you let *eros* control your lovemaking.

Focus on *phileo, agape* and *storge* until the time is right for *eros.* Become a whole person so that the lifetime lover that enters your bed is not getting fragments of a person but someone who is fully alive on all the levels of the relationship. How does one get ready for marriage? Focus on three levels of lovemaking but don't arouse level-two love before it is time.

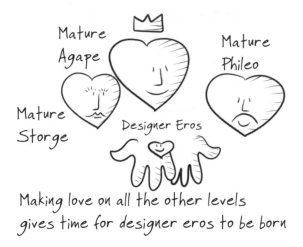

Making love on all the other levels
gives time for designer eros to be born

Finally, what you have already failed? Is it too late? Luke 15 tells the story of the return of the prodigal, the moral failure. There are several key moments in his homecoming. He came to his senses. He returned home. He opened his heart to receive the love of the father who ran down the road to embrace and restore. God runs to us when we walk down that same road. Sexual innocence may be lost forever, but it is never too late for sexual righteousness. With confession and by receiving the mercy and love of the Father, a new life of multilevel lovemaking will be yours and will wash away the folly of the past. For *agape* lovemaking is, as the lovers sang, stronger than death and more powerful than the grave.

Thinking It Through

1. This chapter suggests that sex and love reach their highest level only in multilevel lovemaking, that is, when two people commit to four levels of lovemaking: spiritual union, deep friendship, loving one another's families and physical intimacy. As you consider the Scriptures discussed—Proverbs 5, Song of Songs and Ephesians 5—which passage makes the strongest case to you about multilevel lovemaking? Why?

2. Multilevel lovemaking is a unique bond meant to be enjoyed in one covenant relationship that lasts a lifetime. How much does this view align with your own current thoughts about and experience of sex, love and lifelong commitment? What are the points of agreement? The points of disagreement?

3. Review the four models of moral decision making in Romans 14. Which of these voices do you hear the loudest in your head? Which ones have most affected your decisions about love and sex? How effective has your model been in leading to fully alive lovemaking? Do you need an upgrade to your decision making? What might that look like?

4. The call of the singers tells us that multilevel lovemaking is a political act in a hedonistic world that often sees sex and love as recreational. Do you agree or disagree with this idea? What kind of change might happen in your circle of influence if you practiced the singers' call to lovemaking?

5. What application might this chapter have for a friend or relative who has a same-sex orientation? What help for their journey?

Taking Action

1. Proverbs 5 contains this challenge: "Your spring water is for you and you only, not to be passed around among strangers. Bless your fresh-flowing fountain! Enjoy the wife you married as a young man! Lovely as an angel, beautiful as a rose—don't ever quit taking delight in her body. Never take her love for granted!" (vv. 17-19 *The Message*). Over the next thirty days, if you are married, plan a number of activities that would help you use a multi-level lovemaking strategy to fight for delight in your husband or wife.

chapter nine

The Isaiah Call to Wow

The Pursuit of Happiness

Our pursuit of work-life balance has taken us deep into the story of the Bible. Lady Wisdom has called us to a life of primary play in which we playfully delight in whatever we do, whomever we do it with, and all because of what we see happening wherever we look—an almighty and all loving Father making all things new. To experience this life of playful delight I need to get folly out of my head and heart. Biblical thinking is the key to this transformation of the mind and soul. Abraham's call to believe, the Exodus call to freedom, David's call to relationships and the singers' call to lovemaking are all part of that new perspective on work-life balance. But the unexamined premise behind all of this is our desire for happiness. The dream of happiness is one of humanity's oldest and most elusive dreams.

The Thinker contemplating the various paths to happiness

After centuries in which happiness study was the exclusive province of theologians and philosophers, a shift has taken place. In the last twenty years positive psychology, a movement within the behavioral sciences, has made important contributions to our understanding of happiness. Students at our most elite institutions cram the classrooms of courses devoted to happiness. A leading voice among this new generation of happiness scientists is New York University's Jonathan Haidt.

In his book *The Happiness Hypothesis,* Haidt looks at a number of the factors that make people happy.[1] Genes play a role, and external conditions may play a minor role. Values are very important. One of the surprising factors Haidt focuses on, given his atheism, is what he calls "divinity." He writes that people who experience "elevation," who feel inspired and sense the sacredness of life, tend to cope with adversity better than those without such sensibilities. He reiterates the research that shows that religious people tend to be happier than their non-religious counterparts. One of the benefits of a religious life is a having a story that makes sense of adversity. Haidt cites research that indicates the power of "making sense of life" through a positive narrative, especially in times of crisis or

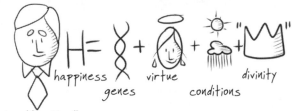

Dr Jonathan Haidt's research on happiness gives a strong role to "divinity," an overarching story that makes sense of life

The call to wow is an encounter with God's mission that moves our little "me" stories into the larger story of "we"

trauma, as an important factor in people recovering and expanding their happiness. When we experience awe in an encounter with a vastness that exceeds our expectations or categories, our values and life narratives change and expand and become more useful in explaining the unexplainable things of life. Linking our little stories to a story of cosmic scope seems to be one of the golden keys to happiness.

Lady Wisdom notes the role of linking little and large narratives in Proverbs 9:10, "The fear of the LORD is the beginning of wisdom, and knowledge of the Holy One is understanding." This is her call to wow, to an encounter with the Almighty that inspires fear and awe. Through this encounter we feel our small stories becoming a part of the greater story of God himself.

Defining Worship

What is this wow encounter that is the key to happiness? For some the word "wow" may seem cheesy. After all, if we're talking about worship, then an everyday expression like "wow" hardly seems appropriate. But "wow" deserves a place in our discussion of worship. The expression "wow" actually comes from Scotland where it may have evolved from "I vow," a solemn act of sacred commitment.

Anne Lamott can help us with the idea of wow. She writes about prayer as three basic conversations with God. Help prayers are the most common. Thanks prayers are a slightly smaller percentage of prayer. The wow prayers are praise, but praise that is not intended to be routine. Lamott elaborates: "The third great prayer, Wow, is often offered with a gasp, a sharp intake of breath, when we can't think of another way to capture the sight of shocking beauty or destruction, of a sudden unbidden insight, or a flash of grace."[2]

Anne Lamott argues that of the three
great prayers, wow prayers are in
short supply. We need to encounter
God's shocking beauty and surprising grace.

The Bible is full of wow prayers. The Psalms and Revelation are just two books full of wow prayers. There are many others as well. My favorite wow prayer is Isaiah's call to wow in chapter 6 of his story. As we eavesdrop on this prayer, we discover that the call to wow is a summons to surprise fueled by the beauty of God and his new creation project.

Isaiah 6 and the Call to Wow

When Isaiah entered the temple that day, the skies were full of birds of prey. King Uzziah had just been zapped with leprosy and died in the temple for trying to play the role of a priest. His death couldn't have happened at a worse time. Assyria, the Klingon empire of its day, was as savage as it was large, and was sweeping south toward Jerusalem. It is not hard to imagine Isaiah feeling depressed and disillusioned as he walked into the worship service on that particular sabbath.

What happened next would change his life. What he saw in a flash of grace and revelation left him sprawled on the ground. What did he see that created one of the greatest wow moments in all of biblical history?

I'll let him tell it in his own words:

In the year that King Uzziah died, I saw the Lord, high and exalted, seated on a throne; and the train of his robe filled the temple. Above him were seraphim, each with six wings: With two wings they covered their faces, with two they covered their feet, and with two they were flying. And they were calling to one another:

"Holy, holy, holy is the LORD Almighty;
    the whole earth is full of his glory."

At the sound of their voices the doorposts and thresholds shook and the temple was filled with smoke. (Isaiah 6:1-4)

This was Isaiah's big wow, and it centered not just on what he saw but also on what he heard. There were two parts to what he heard: a holy wow and a glory wow. Let's begin with the holy wow.

Isaiah's call to wow centered on what he saw &
heard. First was the holy wow and second
was the glory wow.

The Holy Wow

Isaiah saw the King of the universe, the God of mission, high and exalted and surrounded by a group of angels, wings wrapped around them like sunglasses, in the ecstasy of a song. "Holy, holy, holy," the song began.

What is "holy"? Holiness is a moral beauty so distinct and rare that it is like nothing on earth. It is who God is, infinite moral beauty. God is separated from anything ugly, sinful, evil or broken. He is pure, unadulterated, infinite love. The Hebrew language uses repetition as a superlative. If you wanted to say something was the heaviest thing you had ever lifted you would say it was "heavy, heavy." If you wanted to say that a certain girl was the most gorgeous woman you had ever seen you would say she was "gorgeous, gorgeous." Isaiah would have heard the "holy, holy, holy" as the highest superlative possible. God is the most beautiful beauty of all the beauties imaginable. But what was this beauty that God had to such an infinite degree?

Isaiah lived near the end of the Jewish theocratic experiment. Israel, the sons and daughter of Abraham and his *baraka* partnership, was failing to be a blessing to the nations, failing to bring people, work, love, life and nations fully to life. They were in a death spiral. King Uzziah's horrid death was but one more proof that the plane was going down.

In the midst of these circumstances, Isaiah, in the nadir of Israelite political power, is shown how the world really works. The veil of history is pulled back to show that earthly powers do not run the world; beauty does. Swords don't have the last say; love does. Contrary to Nietzsche, truth is not ugly but downright beautiful. Jonathan Edwards, like few theologians I know, thought long and hard about God and beauty.[3] For him beauty came in three varieties.

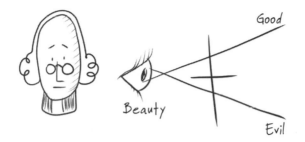

For Jonathan Edwards the highest beauty
is moral beauty. And the highest moral beauty
is the harmony of opposites

The first is simple beauty—symmetry. Symmetry occurs when everything is balanced, in perfect form. An artist who drew one side of a face distorted and the other normal would be breaking the law of symmetry, and most people would judge his work to be ugly. The beauty of the universe in Genesis 1 is a beauty of symmetry. There is no ugly distortion to mar the perfect balance of God's good world.

The second type of beauty is complex beauty. This is a harmony of opposites. Only a great artist can take the ugly bits of life and put them on a canvas with the opposite elements of beauty and truth and bring about a finished painting in which even the ugly has contributed to the overall beauty. Complex beauty produces the biggest wows in life. For Edwards, God was complex beauty. This is not the *Star Wars* version of God in which he has a dark side to go along with his light side. For Edwards, the beauty of God is his ability to absorb the ugly and transform it. God is a being whose beauty is such that when he encounters death he will produce life. His is a beauty so rare that when he encounters ugly he turns it into something grand and glorious. This is not just a little conjuring trick God has learned running the universe. This complex beauty is his essence.

The third beauty for Edwards was moral beauty, or love for persons. Moral beauty is beyond physical beauty. It can be simple—a kind act, a smile to a stranger—or it can be complex: forgiving enemies, dying for someone else, taking someone else's evil and turning it into beauty. For Edwards, God was infinite and complex moral beauty. He takes the world of human sin and folly and misery and transforms it through his self-giving love into the most beautiful love story ever told.

Isaiah saw that complex moral beauty in the temple. The God of mission would make everything beautiful. The Assyria thing, the Uzziah thing, the big mess of his world—all would be notes in a symphony so beautiful that we will weep with joy rather than sorrow at its end. On that day in the temple, Isaiah came face to face with infinite and complex moral beauty. He encountered a God who makes everything beautiful. One look (before your eyes went blind)

Isaiah's holy wow: A God of infinite moral beauty is separated from a world devoid of moral beauty but out of love pours his beauty back into the ugliness.

and you saw what God was. Not the problem that humans have been trying to solve but the solution to the messiness and the miseries of human life. God is a pure, burning flame of loving beauty that will make everything, absolutely everything, beautiful in time. All the young prophet could offer was a holy wow.

Which led Isaiah to encounter the glory wow.

The Glory Wow

Isaiah saw a God so good, so beautiful in his love and grace that even angels had to cover their eyes. But that was not all. The angels kept singing. Beyond the beauty of God's essence was the beauty of God's business. Isaiah got to see, in a flash of revelation, what God was doing in history. That flash occurred at the end of the angels' song: "the whole earth is full of his glory." It was not just heaven that was full of his glory but also earth. He saw God filling our dirty, break-your-heart earth with his healing beauty. What is this glory that came shooting out of God's beauty and filled the earth? Genesis 1 tells us. God's glory is simply life. Life in all of its fullness. Life in all of its diversity. Life, life and more life. God's glory is his infinite, creative and unstoppable action to produce, sustain and renew all of life.

Let's zoom in on this point a little bit. In Genesis 1 we are introduced to God for the first time. He speaks and then life happens. We watch while God makes everything come alive. There was nothingness to begin with and then chaos and void. And then, before we could look at our programs, he makes the Rift Valley in Kenya, the Swiss Alps and the surf in San Diego. He makes the Serengeti, the Grand Canyon, the California redwoods, the Big Dipper and a million other universes that for all we know may be bigger and better than ours. He makes the kingfisher dive and the orca leap and Adam and Eve make love. He makes trees that explode with life-giving fruit, stars that explode with life-giving light and waterfalls that explode with life-giving water. And suddenly we see his glory. The glory of God is a world fully alive.

The glory wow: God's glory is creating life. He is now pouring all of his beauty and glory into making all things fully alive.

Isaiah's dark thoughts about a God who breaks his promises, who lets his kings die and allows his people to fall into slavery under cruel empires vanish like smoke in this moment of wow. Isaiah sees his nation and his world teeming with life. Isaiah gets the song. God is not doing a death thing; he is doing a life thing. In his surprise and wonder, Isaiah's lips form the involuntary response of every human being who has ever been surprised by joy. He says wow.

Isaiah spent the rest of his life unpacking this moment of wow. He wanted to catch every ray of this new shining vision of life and resurrection that was about to dawn on the earth. In chapter 9 of his prophecy we see dawn's first light in the birth of a Son upon whose shoulders the governments of the world will rest and who will rule those governments forever. A Jewish king, the Messiah, so strongly hinted at since the days of Abraham, starts to come into focus. Chapter 11 reveals that that Davidic king will be full of the Spirit of God, giving him incomparable knowledge and wisdom to rule. He will judge evil and reward good. In chapter 32, after several chapters of "woes" on the nations around Israel and groups within Israel, Isaiah returns to the wow of a king of justice who will establish a kingdom of equity and fairness without parallel in human history. In chapter 42 the Davidic king is given a new name, the servant of the Lord. God said, "I will put my Spirit on him, and he will bring justice to the nations" (42:1). In chapters 52 and 53 Isaiah records that this king will be highly exalted among the nations, but only after being killed as an offering of atonement for the people and then raised from the dead.

> Yet it was the LORD's will to crush him and cause him to suffer,
>   and though the LORD makes his life an offering for sin,
> he will see his offspring and prolong his days,
>   and the will of the LORD will prosper in his hand.
> After he has suffered,
>   he will see the light of life and be satisfied.
>
> **ISAIAH 53:10-11**

Isaiah 60 records that the people of the king will enter a golden age so unprecedented that all the kings of the world will stream into Zion and lay their riches at Zion's feet, so desperately will they want a piece of the power, prosperity and life of the people of God under the world's last and greatest King.

The ceaseless care of Zion's king for the nations is rhapsodized in chapter 61. The Davidic king is ever at work, moving among his people and meeting every need. He cries out,

> *The Spirit of the Sovereign Lord is on me,*
> *because the Lord has anointed me*
> *to proclaim good news to the poor.*
> *He has sent me to bind up the brokenhearted,*
> *to proclaim freedom for the captives*
> *and release from darkness for the prisoners,*
> *to proclaim the year of the Lord's favor*
> *and the day of vengeance of our God,*
> *to comfort all who mourn,*
> *and provide for those who grieve in Zion—*
> *to bestow on them a crown of beauty*
> *instead of ashes,*
> *the oil of joy*
> *instead of mourning.*
>
> **ISAIAH 61:1-3**

Isaiah ends his book sharing yet one more detail of what he had seen in the temple on that day of wow. All the nations will join Israel, and together they will enjoy a new creation. In 66:22 he writes in words that echo the song of the angels, "'As the new heavens and the new earth that I make will endure before me,' declares the Lord, 'so will your name and descendants endure.'" People and places, nations and the cities—all will be made beautiful and fully alive once again. Hands go up in the air in *fiero*. Wow.

The New Jerusalem

It is not just Isaiah who couldn't get over his day of wonder in the temple. The rest of the writers of the Bible never got over it either. Scripture continues to build on Isaiah's vision. The slow and steady march of wow reaches its climax with the apostle John and the closing chapters of his Revelation. In the last two chapters of his vision of the future, John picks up on themes introduced by Isaiah. He sees the God of mission and the mission of God fulfilled in history.

In chapters 21 and 22 we see an *earth fully alive*. We see the clear-as-crystal river of life running riot through a world turned into a massive green city. The tree of life is everywhere growing along the river's edge. It is an urbanized world in which development is the ally of the green world, and the green world is the glory of the city.

In this new Jerusalem we see *hearts fully alive with delight*. Folly's brain is gone. Minds and hearts are liberated. So full is the direct delight in God that there are no churches to be seen anywhere. There is no temple. Why no church structures in the new creation? We won't need these structures to refocus heart and mind on God and wean them from the world. God will be so fully and completely the object of delight that idolatry is impossible.

In this new Jerusalem we see *the ekklesia of God fully alive*. No death, no evil, no disease, no sin will ever mar the beauty of the church, pictured here as the bride of Christ. Composed of every people group and speaking every language known to humanity, the people of God will be complete. The broken body of Christ, which for centuries was rent by disunity, discord and divisions, will be fully alive with unity, beauty and wholeness.

In this new creation we see *all the nations fully alive with health and wholeness*. The tree of life in chapter 22 is full of leaves that yield the most amazing medicine ever known—complete healing of the nations from all the horrors of war, disease, poverty, prejudice, misrule, injustice and enslavement.

In Revelation 21 & 22 the mission of God is finished, all things fully and forever alive

The new Eden that is coming will be a world fully alive because there will only be life. All death will be destroyed. All bodies resurrected. On that day there will be a total and permanent humiliation of Admiral Death. He will be shown for what he truly is, the greatest king of fools. He thought his reign over human life was forever and total. He thought he had the last word. Isaiah and Abraham knew better though. Where God is, there must be life. When God is telling the story, it must end in life. God's mission turns all of history into a *baraka* story where life comes out of death. And so death's smile will at last be wiped off his skeletal face as every last man, woman and child is bodily raised and given new resurrection bodies. And the first act of these newly re-embodied

Death's smile will be wiped from its face when the king resurrects all things. Death itself will die.

people will be to fall flat on the ground in front of Isaiah's Davidic king who brings beauty from ashes. Some will rise for judgment due to a persistent and defiant folly that has made them eternally incapable of delighting forever in the beauty of the King. They will begin the slow journey into a moral monsterhood from which there is no return. They fall to the ground before the Messiah out of the wow of terror rather than wonder.

How can such ugliness coexist in a world of such beauty? God's beauty is a complex beauty, able to create a beautiful story even when there are ugly parts. If Tolkien could create a fantasy world of orcs, Mordor and the monsters of Sauron and still wow the world with the glories of Middle Earth redeemed, then God will have little trouble doing the same. But that is not the real story. In complex beauty the ugly bits are still ugly but they become part of a story and canvas of such beauty that they no longer detract from the wonder of the whole. Because the whole earth will be filled with the glory of God. Because

The project of modernity is a Babel project largely irrelevant to the mission of God

beauty wins. This total and utter defeat of sin and death at the end of history is all because of the Davidic king, the Messiah who can only bring life.

Please note what is not said in Isaiah and in John's vision. The new creation is not brought in by science or modernity or capitalism. Not by democracy or

NATO or the United Nations or the World Bank. Not by tyrants or technocrats. The entire Babel project of the Enlightenment, with its grand but flawed illusion of a perfect reason wielded by perfect humans producing a perfect world, has nothing to do with the real transformation of the world. Modernity, at least in its secular forms, is largely irrelevant to an earth and to a people becoming fully alive through a messianic king sent from God.

Gnosticism and the Curse of Super-Spirituality

At this point some might object: what about heaven? What about leaving this world and going to be with our Savior? What about the rapture where we are caught up to meet Jesus in the sky and return with him to heaven as disembodied, floating spirits and transparent souls?

This objection highlights the main reason modern Christians have trouble seeing the wow that Isaiah saw. The objection springs from a little heresy called Gnosticism. In the world-weary Roman Empire of the second century, a significant segment of the growing Christian movement fell into the pit of destructive super-spirituality. It is one thing when the gospel of the Messiah is translated and unleashed in the idiom of a new culture. It is quite another thing when that gospel is thrown away in favor of an exaggerated supernaturalism that has no appetite for a transformed earth. This latter view is Gnosticism, the belief that the purpose of Christianity was to help people escape from their bodies, escape from the earth, escape from life. Spirits liberated to become part of the ocean of being was the pleasing dream of the Gnostic believer. Isaiah's vision would have been hell for the Gnostic, eliciting wows of horror instead of praise.

Gnosticism spread rapidly through the church of the Mediterranean world

Gnosticism rejects
the Isaiah call to wow
 and sees Christianity as
an escape from earth,
an escape from death,
and an escape from life.

for several centuries. It may be the most difficult spiritual and theological battle Christianity has faced. The church eventually won this battle, at least officially. But like all battles, it left scars even on the victors.

We see Gnostic scars in our songs that talk about "one fine morning, . . . I'll fly away," as though we were made for a soulish existence in a disembodied state. The Bible is clear that such a condition is only temporary and that our true home is a physical body standing on a transformed earth.

A life-denying gnosticism sometimes
comes through in our songs and funerals

We see Gnostic scars in our funerals when we speak of the dearly departed being in "their final resting place." The only final resting place is an earth fully alive with the glory of the Eden God. The final rest for believers is standing on that fully alive earth, wind in our faces, sun in our eyes, warm resurrected bodies of those we love all around us, feeling the full force of Eden for the first time. Fighting Gnosticism within and without is an essential part of the genuine wow experience.

Work and Wow

Isaiah's wow encounter does not end with the song of the seraphs. God speaks and asks Isaiah to join him in his mission, in the *baraka* project of bringing full life to the whole earth. Isaiah goes through the cycle of wow. He must confess his sins. He must receive cleansing from God. He must rise to his feet and join God in his mission in a world that is not yet Eden.

After he rises to his feet Isaiah feels the hard slap of the words in 6:11. What will it be like working toward the new creation? Will every day be sweeter than the day before? Will I see progress all along the way? Maybe or maybe not. Working for wow in the world means things may get worse before they get better. It means we may roll the rock up the hill only to see it roll all the way down again, just before we reach the top. Wow at work is Penelope of Greek mythology, happily unraveling her needlepoint at the end of each day because her real job was living, working and playing for the return of her beloved Ulysses. Wow at work may mean working in the middle of a cultural or economic war that rages until everything is dead (6:11). Isaiah reports this shocking news when he says,

> *The country will look like pine and oak forest*
> *with every tree cut down—*
> *Every tree a stump, a huge field of stumps.*
> *But there's a holy seed in those stumps.*
> **ISAIAH 6:13** *THE MESSAGE*

In the midst of a cultural crater of ashes we get to plant and water a wondrous seed. When things die around us, all we will have to hold on to is the holy seed of the messianic good news—that God will raise all things from the dead. That all that is lost will be found. This death is not the negation of the vision of the new Eden; it is the necessary precondition. God plants his Jesus seed of new creation in the ashes of the old. He never gives up on this creation, but he does not build on our Babel projects either. All the towers will come down. But while the towers are crumbling, the tree of life grows. It pops, blade by blade, through the crumbled sidewalks of our ruined Babels and grows into

In a world of death we get to playfully plant
the seeds of hope as we work for the wow

a tall tree. That small green blade, the Davidic King, not only died for our sins and rose bodily from the dead to begin the new creation but also now rules everything that happens on earth from his place at God's right hand as he steers history toward the new heavens and the new earth. Theologians call this the ascension of Jesus. And while we don't yet get to the see the new Jerusalem, we do get to hold the hand of its King every day as we play for the kingdom in a world awaiting its resurrection.[4]

Back to Happiness: Unleashing the Waterfall of Wow

Jonathan Haidt, the self-proclaimed atheist psychologist, thinks that everyone needs "divinity," a vision of the sacred, to maximize happiness. Isaiah agrees. What does that mean for us and our calling?

Learn to start every day with wow. My wife, Lois, reminded me this morning of Proverbs 1:7, "The fear [wow] of the LORD is the beginning of knowledge." You really can't have wisdom without wow. We would not hear God's call to life if we first did not believe he was a God of life. So what does the call of wow mean for our calling? It means we must start the day in wow if we are going to spend the day in wisdom playing for the kingdom. We talk of quiet times and morning devotions. These are important disciplines of the Christian life. But they are not ends in themselves; they are means to an end. The end is always wow. I read the Word to see the mission of God and the God of mission. I sing to fill my soul with hope in the Eden that is coming. I pray my prayers of help and thanks out of the deeper prayer of wow in a God who makes all things new and does all things well. I need to begin with Isaiah 6 before I can live in Proverbs 8.

Learn to bring wow to work. We finish our morning wow time and we go to work. We battle the traffic, dodge potholes, spill our coffee on our new shirt, fight for parking and finally arrive at the office only to find that Dame Folly has arrived before us. Folly's fingerprints are everywhere. Her little box of horrors is leaning against the ficus plant. Her brainwashed minions look dazed and distracted. Her old lies are circulating around the water cooler and in the first emails of the morning. But we don't despair. Into this charred and poisoned soil we plant the holy seed of the good news of the Davidic King returning soon and ruling now. We don't necessarily preach it, but we must live it. We love our enemies. We create a culture of peace in the office. We do our work playfully. We play for the kingdom in all of life. And then we watch that holy seed become a blade of grass that breaks through the concrete. We watch that seed become a small branch that gives shade to the weary. We watch that seed grow into a tree of life full of new love, new play and new work. And people take notice. Suddenly our dead-end jobs are now leading to the new creation. The play of wow is a way of working that will change the world.

Learn to bring wow to church. We need to bring this spirit of playful wow to worship as well. I know we go to church seeking the wow, but we won't always find it there. Sometimes we must make it happen. Maybe the seats are uncomfortable. Maybe the worship team is off-key or too loud. Maybe the sermon is off-topic or too chaotic to follow. Maybe the kids in the row behind you are driving you crazy. Play the wow game right there and then. Close your eyes and sing silently, *Holy, holy, holy, wow, wow, wow, the whole earth is becoming fully alive through my beautiful God and his beautiful Son.* And do an imaginary walk-through of the new Eden, an earth fully alive. A New York or a Nairobi fully alive. The world of art and music fully alive. The world of government and economics fully alive. The world of love, friends and families, fully, gloriously, bodily, eternally alive with the fullness of God. The dead raised. Nations healed. Idolatry gone. Imagine the people around you in resurrected bodies (keep the clothes on, please!), fully alive in their transformed work, play and love. Imagine yourself experiencing these wonders. And I dare you not to smile right there in the third pew next to that crying kid, to try to keep your lips from forming that most spectacular of all one-syllable words: *Wow*.

Thinking It Through

1. The chapter begins by citing Jonathan Haidt's research on happiness. Do you agree or disagree with his assessment that people who experience "elevation," who sense the sacredness of life, tend to cope with adversity better than those without such sensibilities? Have you seen examples of this in your own life?

2. Isaiah's vision is one of the most powerful pictures of God as an almighty Father at work all around us making everything new. Reread Isaiah 6 and note Isaiah's wow responses to the vision. Which response would help you cultivate that spirit of primary play that would make wisdom work possible?

3. Isaiah's call to wow requires a new sense of beauty, moving from simple beauty (symmetry) to complex beauty (the harmony of opposites). As you review your life, can you find examples of both kinds of beauty? In retrospect, which is more satisfying?

4. The call to wow is the call to worship and delight in a God who is making all things new. Everything and everyone will be resurrected and utterly trans-

formed. Compare this view and its potential to generate hope and happiness to naturalistic worldviews that insist that this world is all there is and that it will eventually end in the collapse of a contracting universe. Why do so many people believe the doomed-earth view is true and the transformed-earth view is false? Where are you on the spectrum of glory and gloom about your future and the future of all things? What decisions do you need to make to move toward a life of wow?

5. Gnosticism is identified as one of the enemies of the ecstasy Isaiah experienced. How have you struggled with Gnostic elements in your own spirituality? How might Isaiah's vision help you overcome this problem?

Taking Action

1. The chapter closes with three suggested applications. Which of the three is the most relevant to where you're at right now? Why? What specific actions might you take to put Isaiah's call to wow into effect? Using the game dynamics and the pomodoro technique described in chapter two, how could you build wow into the game of daily life? Practice this today.

chapter ten

The Jesus Call to Dance

Finally. **You knew that we would** have to get to Jesus at some point. Not only is he the most revered and most controversial character in all of history but he is also the center of Christian faith and the climax of the biblical story. Jesus is the central focus of Christian worship and Christian practice. But for many emerging adults, the model of work-life balance that Jesus displayed in his thirty-three years on earth doesn't really count. Not that Jesus did anything wrong. It's just that Jesus is so unusual. For Christians, Jesus is God among us. How can I really hope to follow the example of Jesus when he obviously had a whole set of superpowers not available to the rest of us?

It's time we rediscovered Jesus. In his earthly life and ministry Jesus only used resources available to all of us. His way of working, playing and loving is a way that should be emulated and can be emulated if we will but hear his call.

But what is his call? When we read the Gospels, we see Jesus issuing many calls. Here are a few of the more famous ones:

1. In Matthew 28:19-20, sometimes called the Great Commission, we read Jesus' call to mission, exhorting us to "go and make disciples of all nations."

2. We have the call to rest in Matthew 11:28: "Come to me, all you who are weary and burdened, and I will give you rest."

3. We have the call to love in Mark 12:30-31: "'Love the Lord your God with all your heart and with all your soul and with all your mind and with all your strength.' The second [greatest commandment] is this: 'Love your neighbor as yourself.'" Jesus himself referred to the call to love as the greatest commandment.

4. We have the entire Sermon on the Mount in Matthew 5–7 with various commands such as loving one's enemies, turning the other cheek and being perfect as God is perfect.

And many more. Which do we choose? I would like to suggest a call that is often neglected, buried away in the thick underbrush. It's found in John 15:5: "I am the vine; you are the branches. If you remain in me and I in you, you will bear much fruit; apart from me you can do nothing." While the call to love is the most important command, the call to abide in Christ is the most important

John 15:5 as the key call

The call to abide in Christ is the call to dance, to have the life of God so flowing within that we become relevant to his mission

means to that end. This call to remain, or to live inside of God as fully as he lives inside of us, is *the call to dance,* the call to be so full of the flow of God within us that we are able to be relevant to his mission around us.

In this chapter we want to hear this call as the key to all the calls of Jesus and, for that matter, all the other calls of the Bible. We'll look at three parts of this dance that leads to life:

- The Lord of the dance: The one who leads the way to human flourishing

- The call to the dance: The secret life of Jesus Christ

- Joining the dance: Hearing the call and learning the moves

We start with the Lord of the dance to make sure we are clear on the identity of the one who calls.

The Lord of the Dance

Who is Jesus Christ? Historians, theologians, philosophers and sages have all struggled to answer that question with any kind of consensus, but for the writers of the Gospels, the answer was clear as day. All of them address the question of his identity and answer it within their opening chapters. And they all say pretty much the same thing: he is the Davidic king prophesied by Isaiah to bring about the new creation. Even John, who opens his Gospel by identifying Jesus as the word of God and as the God of the word, still echoes Isaiah when he says that the light has come into the world and the darkness has not understood it (John 1:4-5; compare to Isaiah 9:2). In our story of calling, Jesus is the king of wow who fulfills the Isaiah 6 vision of making everything and everyone fully alive. The Gospels present Jesus as the King of life, the one whom Isaiah saw as filling the whole world with new life, which is the glory of God. Jesus is Isaiah's great champion of the mission of God.

We looked over Isaiah's shoulder in the temple when he saw the complex beauty of a holy God and an earth full of his glory, a world fully alive. When the Gospel writers looked at Jesus they saw the same thing, the world's first fully alive human being. Consider the following snapshots of Jesus from each of the Gospels.

Like Isaiah, the Gospel writers saw the birth of Jesus as the birth of the king of wow (see Isaiah 9). In Luke 1:31-33 we read the angel's explanation to Mary of who her Son would be and what he would accomplish: "You will conceive and give birth to a son, and you are to call him Jesus. He will be great and will be called the Son of the Most High. The Lord God will give him the throne of his father David, and he will reign over Jacob's descendants forever; his kingdom will never end." Jesus is born as the king Isaiah saw.

Like Isaiah, the Gospel writers saw Jesus' public ministry as the anointing of a new king with the power of the Spirit (see Isaiah 11). In Mark 1:10-11 we read: "As Jesus was coming up out of the water, he saw heaven being torn open and the

Isaiah 9 ➔ Luke 1

The King is born

Isaiah 11 ➔ Mark 1

The King filled with the Spirit of God

Spirit descending on him like a dove. And a voice came from heaven: 'You are my Son, whom I love; with you I am well pleased.'" This is the same Spirit that we have already met in Genesis 1, "moving over the waters," producing the original Eden, the place of human flourishing. Here in the Gospel account of Jesus receiving the Spirit for his royal rule a new Eden is being born. "Just as the original creation of the world was a project of the triune God," writes Tim Keller, "the redemption of the world, the rescue and renewal of all things that is beginning now with the arrival of the King, is also a project of the triune God."[1]

Like Isaiah, the Gospel writers saw Jesus' new kingdom as one of justice and love, in which he healed the sick, restored the fallen, fed the hungry and raised the dead (see Isaiah 32; cf. Luke 6:19; John 6:10-14). When we put the King and his kingdom of justice and mercy first in our loyalties and loves, we will experience the full prosperity of his rule. All *baraka* will break loose (see Matthew 6:33).

Like Isaiah, the Gospel writers saw Jesus as the Servant King who would sacrifice all for the flourishing of all people (see Isaiah 42; cf. John 13:1-17). No

Isaiah 32 → Luke 6, John 6, Matthew 6

The King of Justice and healing

Isaiah 42 → John 13

The Servant King

task is too hard or humble for the servant of servants to do. He will pay whatever price must be paid to make his people clean and whole again.

Like Isaiah, the Gospel writers saw Jesus' death and resurrection as critical to the success of the mission of God presented in the Old Testament and the inauguration of the new creation (see Isaiah 53). In Luke 24:45-47 we read: "Then he opened their minds so they could understand the Scriptures. He told them, 'This is what is written: The Messiah will suffer and rise from the dead on the third day, and repentance for the forgiveness of sins will be preached in his name

The King who died and rose again   The King who rules the world

to all nations, beginning at Jerusalem.'" He is the suffering Servant King who died and rose again.

Like Isaiah, the Gospel writers saw Jesus' ascension not as disappearance but as revealing his control of all power on earth (see Isaiah 60). All the kings of the earth were but putty in his messianic hands. As Jesus declares in Matthew 28:18,

"All authority in heaven and on earth has been given to me." He would manipulate the kings of history for the purposes of his mission.

Like Isaiah, the Gospel writers saw that Jesus' mission was to take death,
despair and ashes and turn them into the garments of praise and the beauty of
new life (see Isaiah 61). John writes that Jesus declared to his friends Mary and
Martha, just prior to raising their brother from the dead, "I am the resurrection
and the life. The one who believes in me will live, even though they die; and
whoever lives by believing in me will never die" (John 11:25-26). He is the
Davidic king of beauty and life.

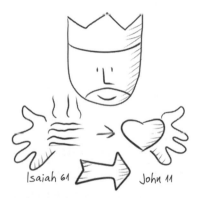

The King who brings beauty from ashes

the King of the New Creation

Like Isaiah, the Gospel writers saw that Jesus inaugurated a kingdom that
would eventually become the new creation where everything would be made
new (see Isaiah 66). When John recorded the first miracle of Jesus as turning
water to wine at the wedding, he was pointing to the one who will transform
the bland water of a world of folly into the sparkling champagne of a new Eden.

Jesus himself called this the *palingenesia,* or the time when he will make everything and everyone fully alive. Jesus speaks in Matthew 19:28 of the kingdom program as "the renewal of all things."

These writers saw what Isaiah saw. But they also saw more. They saw that the Davidic king who now rules the whole show from a position of total power issues one particular call that is the key to all of the others. What is this call and what does it mean?

The Call to Dance: The Secret Life of Jesus Christ

How did Jesus do all that he did? How did he fulfill the Isaiah vision so completely and powerfully? The answer that John gives us is surprising: Jesus is a very good dancer. To see this we need to look at the dance of God, the call of calls, in the Gospel of John.

I am not being metaphorical when I speak of the call to dance as the call of calls and the skill of Jesus as the greatest dancer in the cosmos. This call goes to the deepest heart of the Christian faith, the triune God, and the love that is behind creation, judgment and the renewal of all things. C. S. Lewis describes this secret life of God: "In Christianity God is not a static thing . . . but a dynamic, pulsating activity, a life, almost a kind of drama. Almost, if you will not think me irreverent, a kind of dance."[2]

Lewis was not the first to suggest the secret life of God as dance. The ancient Christian theologians spoke of the Trinity as a dance using the Greek term *perichoresis,* literally, to flow around or dance around. We get our word for choreography from this Greek word. What they meant by the term was mutual indwelling or interpenetration. Though this may sound strange to our ears it is really a word picture of partners in a dance, in which each person is distinct but their intertwined bodies and movement is so lyrical that they seem to flow in and through one another. The Trinity is a family of love and constant action, continually being filled with the infinite love of the others and inexhaustibly filling the others with their love. Keller elaborates: "The Father, the Son, and the Spirit are pouring love and joy and adoration into the other, each one serving the other. They are infinitely seeking one another's glory, and so God is infinitely happy." Why is that signifcant? "And if it's true that this world has been created by this triune God, then ultimate reality is a dance."[3]

Jesus did everything by "dancing," playfully delighting in the "wherever" of the Father and the Spirit

John is the one Gospel writer who describes in detail Jesus' call to dance. As we saw earlier, in John 15:5 Jesus summons us with the call of calls: "I am the vine; you are the branches. If you remain in me and I in you, you will bear much fruit; apart from me you can do nothing." The key word in this call of Jesus is *meno*. It has a wide range of meanings, but if it has a center it is "make yourself at home."

In much of the New Testament the word is used both literally and metaphorically to invite dwelling or making your home in a certain place. *Meno* is not a place you visit but the place you live. It's not the periphery of your life but the center of it. John, writing in his first letter to the churches, expands on the meaning of *meno*: "If anyone acknowledges that Jesus is the Son of God, God lives in them and they in God" (1 John 4:15). In John's understanding, to *meno* is to experience being filled with the life of God and dwelling in God with our lives. In other words, mutual indwelling is the heart of John 15 *meno*.

So, what is this mutual flow of love and life all about? When the world hit Jesus with a need, he didn't meet the need in his own strength. He turned to the Father in glad dependence, and the Father filled the Son with his fullness through the Spirit. Only after Jesus redefined the reality around him as a dance with the Father did he engage the world full of flow, *fiero* and fearlessness. Don't miss the point: *Everything Jesus does to fulfill the mission of God and usher in the new creation he does through playful dancing.*

Let's look at John 1 as an example. There we encounter the great challenge facing Jesus: turning back the darkness that has filled the world. Darkness in John is a lethal mixture of Genesis 1:2 chaos and Genesis 3 folly. Darkness keeps the world, the nations and the individual from becoming fully alive. Jesus comes as light and life to drive out the shadows of chaos and darkness. How does he do it? Through the dance. First, he turns to the Father and redefines his reality as a game they will play together. There is the flow of intimacy with God the Father. In John 1:1-2, John identifies the cosmic warrior as the Word who was with God. Hear the echo with Proverbs 8, where wisdom is the beloved partner at God's side as he makes the universe.

Second, Jesus can fight the darkness because he is full of the servant love that enables him to do anything the Father wants. In John 1:3 we are told that the Word is the one who worked with God to make everything that is made. In addition, he loves being with the Father and loves those the Father loves. He was with God and came into the world to make "children of God" (John 1:12) because the Father loves the lost, and Jesus loves those whom the Father loves. Finally, Jesus delights to exalt the Father by depending on him for everything, even though he is fully God in his own right. This is a loving dependence that has as its purpose the joy of the Son in exalting the Father before the world. We read in John 1:18 that "no one has ever seen God, but the one and only Son, who is himself God and is in closest relationship with the Father, has made him known." In John 1:32 Jesus is given the Spirit of God to empower him for his work in defeating darkness and bringing many children into the kingdom of the Father. He humbly receives this power from the Father not because he needs it but because he delights to depend on the Father and the Spirit as a way of

In John 1, Jesus overcomes the "whatever" of cosmic darkness by delighting in the "wherever" of the Father and Spirit

exalting them. Jesus' ultimate goal was spreading the name and fame of the Father. Through this threefold dance of mutual love, John proclaims, Jesus can turn back to the world and love the whatever and the whomever. This is the love and delight that will overcome the darkness and bring fullness of life and light back into the world.

Don't miss the fact that Jesus' threefold love was freely given. Jesus was fully God. There was no natural inferiority that required Jesus to do any of this. The love of the Son for the Father was motivated not by necessity but by pure freedom and delight. This point is established in John 1 and is woven throughout the rest of the Gospel. I won't point out each instance in which Jesus' full equality with the Father is restated, but please note that it is a key part of the dance.

In John 3 Jesus faces the challenge posed by Nicodemus, who misunderstands Jesus and his purpose. How can someone be transformed? How do people become part of the new creation and enter the mission of God? New creation requires new birth (regeneration by the Spirit; John 3:3-5). Nicodemus saw Jesus as a teacher from God who did works of power. All true as far as it went. Jesus makes it clear, however, that his real identity is Lord of the dance, calling people and transforming people (the new birth) so that they could enter the new-creation mission of God (the kingdom).

How does Jesus help Nicodemus understand the mysteries of God, life and salvation? First, he redefines reality in terms of the Father's almighty love and power. In John 3:13 he declares that "no one has ever gone into heaven except the one who came from heaven," thereby proclaiming his unique, intimate love with the Father. Before Jesus meets Nicodemus's need, he has to delight in the Father at work all around him to make all things new. Jesus is the one who loves to do whatever the Father wants. This includes sacrificial service to the Father. The Son is willing to be sent to his death out of his delight and love for the Father and his love for those whom the Father loves. John 3:16 states, "For God so loved the world that he gave his one and only Son, that whoever believes in him shall not perish but have eternal life." Nicodemus may have wanted just a few tips on how to be a good person, but what he got was an invitation to the dance by the lead dancer.

In John 3, Jesus handled the questions of Nicodemus by a Proverbs 8 partnership with the Father and the Spirit

In John 5 the flow of mutual love is made more explicit. Jesus heals a paralytic and is attacked by the religious leaders for doing this on the sabbath, the day in which every devout Jew was expected to abstain from any kind of work whatsoever (except works of necessity). Jesus argues that for him, healing this man who had suffered with his disability for thirty-eight years was necessary. Jesus' mission was to make everything and everyone fully alive again, so he had to heal the man. Where did he get this mission? The dance. He redefines reality not in terms of the medical needs of the man or the medical resources of the community but rather in Proverbs 8 terms, of an almighty Father at work everywhere around him. He lives inside this flowing circle of mutual love. Not only does he love the Father but "the Father loves the Son" (John 5:20). Out of this mutual, intimate love flows mutual service: "For just as the Father raises the dead and gives them life, even so the Son gives life to whom he is pleased to give it" (John 5:21). Father and Son, intertwined in the dance of love, work together in mutual service to restore life to everything and everyone. Finally, Jesus decided to heal the paralyzed man, he explains to his critics, because the Father honored him with the power to make these kinds of decisions. And Jesus only made the decisions to heal and help if they would in turn honor the Father. "The Father judges no one," Jesus explains, "but has entrusted all judgment to the Son, that all may honor the Son just as they honor the Father. Whoever does not honor the Son does not honor the Father, who sent him" (John 5:22-23).

In John 5 Jesus heals a paralyzed man
and faces the attacks of his critics
by trusting completely in the "wherever"
of his Father

The dance continues in John 6–8 and 10. Jesus explains his preaching, healing and sin-forgiving work as flowing from mutual intimacy with the father (John 6:46; 7:29; 8:29; 10:14-15), mutual service between Father and Son (6:32; 7:28; 8:34-38; 10:17-18), and mutual deference between Father and Son (6:38, 40; 7:16-18; 8:54; 10:24-25). The darkness grows in resistance, but Jesus fights back with the power of flow.

By the time we reach John 14, Jesus is ready to drop the bombshell: *His followers will get to join the dance through the gift of the Spirit flowing in and through them.* This is his parting gift before he ascends to power in the primary plane of existence, heaven, and will be physically separated from them. Though he is leaving, they need not have fear, he says, because the mutual love between Father, Son and Spirit, this joyful, infinite, ecstatic intimacy, service and deference, will now include them. He will give them the Spirit of the dance to flow in and through them. This will not only diminish the loneliness of physical separation but also increase the inner joy of spiritual intimacy as the love of God fills and flows into every part of their being and through them into his world.

They are puzzled by this gift. What does it mean? Will it even work? Why won't Jesus just stay around so things can be as they always were? Jesus assures them this new life of flow will work because it has always worked for him. Jesus' entire life on earth was sustained by his intimacy with the Father. As he explains in John 14:10-11: "Don't you believe that I am in the Father, and that the Father is in me? The words I say to you I do not speak on my own authority. Rather, it is the Father, living in me, who is doing his work. Believe me when I say that I am in the Father and the Father is in me; or at least believe on the evidence of the works themselves." The Spirit will come and give them that same sense of

In John 14 Jesus brings his hurting
disciples into the dance. They now
can enjoy the same relationship with the
Father and the Spirit that he has.

being in the Father and the Father being in them, for this "Spirit of truth" will live "with you and will be in you" (John 14:17-18).

Out of Jesus' delight in the wherever came his delight in the whatever and the whomever. He lived a life of delighting in the other and whatever the other wanted him to do. In the same way, the Spirit will fill the followers with delight in the triune God's presence and will be key to the flow of service that Jesus will continue in them and in the world through them. Jesus is going to "prepare a place for [them]" (John 14:2). It is a place whose path they know well, he says. The place is the transformed earth, and the path to that transformed earth is the work of Jesus as Davidic king. He will build the new creation in them and through them.

> Do not let your hearts be troubled. You believe in God; believe also in
> me. My Father's house has many rooms; if that were not so, would I
> have told you that I am going there to prepare a place for you? And if

I go and prepare a place for you, I will come back and take you to be with me that you also may be where I am. You know the way to the place where I am going. (John 14:1-4)

Jesus is "the way, the truth and the life" (John 14:6), the complete champion to bring us into the dance of infinite, inexhaustible love. His service as a middle man or mediator who will lead the people of God into the fullness of the Father's new Eden project will continue through the Spirit. Jesus lived his whole life exalting the Father through the power of the Spirit, out of delight and not just duty, so he knows the Spirit will do the same for his disciples. The flow of

When we become followers of Jesus we are given the Holy Spirit to fill us with the triple delight of primary play just as Jesus was

deferential love for the Father will continue, flowing out of the Spirit and into his followers. Jesus believes this because the Father has told him so. Everything he is telling them comes from the Father: "These words I say to you I do not speak on my own authority. Rather, it is the Father, living in me, who is doing his work" (John 14:10). The Spirit of Jesus will fill us with the same triple delight that filled the Lord of the dance.

Dancing with the Damned

What about the end of John's story? Why does John, who focuses on the dance of delight more than any other biblical writer, spend half his Gospel focusing on the death of Christ? Doesn't Jesus' death end, or at least interrupt, the dance of God?

This takes us to the central question of the life of Christ and of the Bible itself: What has death got to do with life? What does death have to do with God's *baraka* project of making everything and everyone fully alive? It seems to be a contradiction of his project, if anything.

The death of Jesus is necessary in order for his followers to join the dance because of a little thing called folly. Here is the thing about Dame Folly. Her call to defiance—to take control of our own lives and do what we want, to try to cheat God and death and judgment—is not just persuasive; it is addictive. We have become folly's slaves. And she is as tough as Pharaoh about letting her slaves go. The only exit for folly's fools is death. Either her fools die or someone dies for them. There is no other way out. For the kingdom of folly, time doesn't heal all wounds. It only ends all hope.

This road to nowhere can only be changed if God does something dramatic, and that is what we see in John 19. Down that road of nowhere comes a dancing God with a new twist to the tragic tale of folly's fools. The mutual indwelling of glad intimacy, service and deference continues outside the walls of Jerusalem and up the long climb to the place of the skull, Golgotha. On the cross, Christ changes the dance of God. God's eternal dance has always been between Father, Son and Spirit, three persons in one God whose mutual perfection inspires infinite love, honor and service. In John 19:30, after every manner of insult, humiliation, legal injustice and human torture had been endured, Jesus lifts his head toward heaven and utters the words "It is finished." Was he throwing in the towel? Was he now folly's slave, ending his life in despair? Hardly. The word that Jesus uses, *tetelestai,* is a word not of defeat but of accomplishment. Jesus had used the term when he said, "I have brought you glory on earth by *completing* the work you gave me to do" (John 17:4 NIV 1984). And that is what Jesus is saying on the cross. The work is done, completed, achieved. With his death he completes God's *baraka* project.

How? He completes the dream of Abraham, the cry of the exodus, the promise to David, the wow of Isaiah and the song of the lovers by taking upon himself the curse of folly, sin and death. And by taking on the curse of death himself, he took it off everyone and everything else that it lay over. The great exchange of death for life took place in the death of Christ. The earth will now be renewed as Isaiah foresaw because a death has cleansed the earth (2 Peter 3:10; Revelation 22:1-5). Delight in God rather than folly and idols will be restored because a death has cleansed hearts (Philippians 2:11). The church will be perfected with people from every age, every ethnicity, every class and kind because a death has cleansed humanity of their sin (2 Corinthians 5:21), and the nations will be healed because a death has rid the world of evil and injustice (Isaiah 60; Revelation 22; Romans 8:19-21). God can give *baraka* away to all because Jesus took Babel away from all. As Chris Wright has stated, "The cross was the unavoidable cost of God's mission."[4]

By taking the comprehensive curse of sin, folly & death that lies on all of life Jesus removed it from all of life so that we might have the life of Proverbs 8

When we say that Jesus "took our place" we are saying that he changed the dance of God forever. The mutual indwelling, where the love and delight of each member flowed in and through the other, was exclusive. Anything vile, cursed or dead could not be allowed into the dance of life. But what if the Lord of the dance flowed into the dead and dwelt in the place of death? What if the dead and damned were raised to flow into the heart of God? This transfusion of hearts, this mutual indwelling of deity and damned, means that folly's grip on life was broken. By trading places, Jesus performed a cosmic bypass surgery, in which the contaminated blood of the damned flowed through him and the pure life and love of God flowed through folly's fools. This new circulatory system saves the patients, but it cost the life of the surgeon. The cross created the exchanged life in which we pour all of our folly into him, and he pours all of his infinite love and righteousness and beauty into us. From that day of death onward, the only life we can live, because of mutual indwelling, is an exchanged life.

And so we dance. Faltering at first, tripping as we go, crutches under our arms, we hold on to our partner, all under the smile of our almighty Father and in the arms of his infinite omni-competent Spirit. Full of his flow, we spin around the dance floor. As we spin we go into all the world. We make disciples. We obey. We bring our burdens to God. We love one another as he has loved us. But before the going, before the disciple making, before the resting and the loving, comes the playful dance of God in Christ.

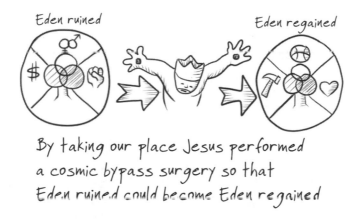

By taking our place Jesus performed a cosmic bypass surgery so that Eden ruined could become Eden regained

Jesus does not stay dead, however. On the third day he is raised bodily from the grave and given a transformed body that cannot die and can move easily between the two major planes of existence, heaven and earth. In his new resurrected state, the Lord of the dance is crowned King of kings and ascends to his throne in the plane of heaven even while his footstool is on the plane of earth (Psalm 2). The dance continues, with the curse on all things being purged by his cleansing death. When the dance is done the new creation will appear and the *baraka* project, perfectly initiated by Christ, will be perfectly concluded by him. The dance of God will fill all time and all space.

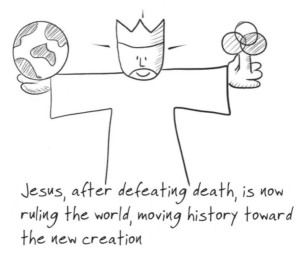

Jesus, after defeating death, is now ruling the world, moving history toward the new creation

The Call to Play and the Call to Dance

John 15:5 is the call to this mutual life of dwelling in the Father's love through Jesus and pouring our "good, bad and ugly" into our champion. This is the dance to which he calls us.

Why is this the call of calls? Because the dance of the Gospels is the play of Proverbs 8. John brings us back to Proverbs 8 and the play of wisdom in the first creation. Lady Wisdom's call to play with and for God in all of life is the dance that we were made for. That play is a threefold delight in the whatever, the whomever and the forever. Jesus' call to the dance of mutual indwelling is the call to play for the kingdom. Wisdom's first delight (the whatever) is seen in

Jesus' love of doing the Father's will, whatever it was, even to the point of death. The call to wisdom's second delight, the whomever, is seen in Jesus' love for the Father's world. To delight in whomever I am doing his work with and for is a call to delight in both the Trinity and the world that is coming home to the Father. Lady Wisdom's call to that third delight, living safely and securely forever in the almighty arms of God who is making all things new, is the Jesus call to gladly depend on the Father and the Spirit for power, provision and protection in all things. Jesus delights in doing everything in his father's loving arms, in a way that gives the Father and the Spirit all the honor and praise.

It should now be clear that the only way we can answer the call to play in all of life is through Christ, the Lord of the dance. Only he can make it possible to join the play of God. When I enter that dance through him, I am filled with the triple delight that overcomes folly, that produces great work, great play, great love. I believe like Abraham. I am free like the Israelites after the exodus. I fight for delight like David and David's God. I experience the wow of Isaiah and the

In Jesus, Wisdom embodied, the call
to dance is Lady Wisdom's call to play

ecstasy of Song of Songs. Jesus is the wisdom of God. He is the key to the call to play because he is the key to the call to dance.

Learning to Dance

When his disciples were getting a little confused about all these things, Jesus gave them four simple instructions they needed to learn to generate the delight necessary to dance their way into the mission of God.

These four steps are found in Luke 9:23: "If anyone would come after me, he must deny himself and take up his cross daily and follow me" (NIV 1984). These words connect with John's call to dance in 15:5, to mutual indwelling, because they teach us the moves we need to stay close to the love that wants to fill us and flow through us, body and soul.

The first dance step is wanting to follow the call of Jesus: "if anyone would come after me." This is a big if. All the hows in the world are useless if there is no desire to dance with Jesus. Folly's fools believe life is found in doing whatever you want with other likeminded friends and cheating death through pleasure or power. Lady Wisdom and her Lord of wisdom call us to another path: following after him. I made this decision many years ago. It has meant joining the dance of God, being filled with his love daily, pouring my garbage into him daily and watching him transform it, letting his life flow in and through me together with other Christians in community. This is a decision that I would encourage each reader to make with all the urgency of life itself.

The second step of the dance is to deny the self. This is not a call to the annihilation of the self or to giving up certain things for Lent or the new year, but rather a call to deny the sovereignty of the self. It is rejection of folly's credo:

"It's my life, I can do what I want." Many cultures of the world are steeped in this folly. To dance with the King requires changing allegiance from the self as supreme to the supremacy of the Lord of the dance. This requires a transfer of ownership and is a decision we must make daily.

The third step is learning to dance with a cross in our hands. This includes learning to endure daily suffering with patience, but it means more than that. To dance is to live a life of exchange, an exchange made possible by the cross. We dance to exchange our need with his supply, our alienation with his love, our infection of folly with his flow of wisdom. Daily practice of the exchanged life is the heart of the dance God calls us to. This is what it means to carry the cross daily.

The final step of the dance of God's mission is to follow Christ. To live as he lived. To die as he died. To love as he loved. This is life in the Spirit. Because of step three, the exchange, we are no longer under the law of sin and death but have been set free to live under the new law of the Spirit and of life (Romans 8:1-2). If we walk in the Spirit we will not follow folly but will walk in the ways

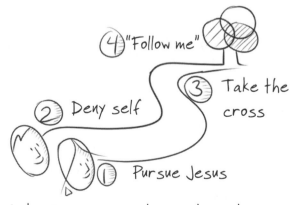

Luke 9:23 gives 4 dance steps to move us toward a life of flow and mission

of the Lord of wisdom. Through the Spirit of God our whole lives are poured into and through the life of the Father and the Son. Through the Spirit of God the whole life of the Father and the Son is poured into me and into his people as a body.

Which call of Jesus? To dance. To dance is to love, to go, to rest. To dance is to change the world.

Thinking It Through

1. This chapter presents the core identify of Jesus as the Davidic king who brought about the wow world foreseen by Isaiah. We grow up with many pictures of Jesus: shepherd, Savior, man of sorrows, countercultural rebel. How might a steady focus on the portrait of Jesus the king presented in the Gospels change your understanding of Christianity, the church and your mission in life?

2. Jesus practiced a special kind of flow that gave him incredible power and grace under pressure. What elements of that flow interest you the most? What are some ways you might practice that flow on campus or in your career?

3. The key to flow is union and mutual indwelling. This relationship with God involves transferring ownership and control of your life from yourself to Jesus Christ. The Holy Spirit takes this transfer and turns it into a living union and communion with Jesus and enables his life to start flowing in and through us. Some of us made aborted transfers perhaps earlier in life. Wisdom calls us to review and renew this transfer in order to live a life of

triple delight. What is the current state of play when it comes to who owns you and controls you? Is it slightly creepy to think of God owning and controlling you? Whose voice are you listening to?

Taking Action

1. Read about the wow. Two books that have helped me understand Jesus as the Davidic king who will make everything and everyone fully alive are Scot McKnight, *The King Jesus Gospel: The Original Good News Revisited* (Grand Rapids: Zondervan, 2010), and N. T. Wright, *How God Became King: The Forgotten Story of the Gospels* (San Francisco: HarperOne, 2012).

chapter eleven

The Acts Call to Change the World

Imagine having this dream. You are standing on a high hill overlooking a city on a vast plain. The city gleams in the sun, making you wonder if it is made of diamonds. The skyline takes your breath away with its towering buildings and matchless architecture. But something is wrong. The longer you look the more you realize that the city is on fire.

Smoke rises from every section of the city. Flames dance above the skyline. One large skyscraper crumbles into ashes before your eyes. You see people leaping to their deaths from high buildings. Crowds of people run from the city, their faces distorted with horror and fear.

As you stare at this scene of chaos and destruction, you hear music. Your eye follows the sound, and you see an odd scene at the city gates: a band of colorfully dressed minstrels, playing music, juggling and dancing, make their way into the smoking city. Their music can just be heard above the cries of victims and the crash of structures. As the odd parade moves into the city limits, something happens to the city. The cries of terror grow silent. The leaping flames subside. The towers of smoke grow smaller. People stop running madly about. Instead they stand and watch as the parade goes by. Some children join the band of minstrels, dancing and laughing as they move through the ruined streets, and the parade of gets bigger.

You watch as the merry band moves through section after section of the troubled city. Everywhere they go they produce the same effect. Where there was chaos, now there is calm. Where there was misery, now there is peace.

By the time the colorful minstrels leave the city, the fires and destruction have ended. The smoke and anarchy have vanished. *Who are these people?* you wonder. *What magical power do they possess?* They entered a doomed city and left it healed and whole.

Your dream is about changing the world, one of the most persistent dreams in human history. People love their revolutions. Long before Christianity was a fixture of our civilization it was a revolution. A small band of spiritual radicals rejecting violence, racism and hate moved through the Roman world and created a quiet revolution. By the time this bottom-up revolution reached the fourth century, the social, political and economic rules of the Roman Empire were radically altered.

In this chapter we will explore the final call of the mission of God: the call to change the world. Work-life balance is not just about self-satisfaction and personal fulfillment. It is also about self-transcendence, finding a cause bigger than ourselves and giving ourselves fully to that good cause. That good and worthy cause, we have seen, is the mission of God. To find ultimate balance in work, play and love means finding our place in the mission of God. Choosing to join God's mission means becoming a wisdom worker who hears and obeys a number of significant calls: the Eden call to playful work, the Abraham call to believe in God's mission, the Exodus call to follow this mission in freedom, and the David call to fight for delight in God and others. The mission of God means the call to wow, the call to lovemaking and the call to the dance. We return to the foundational call, Wisdom's call to play and to show its power to change our world. Only when we join this playful parade that heals our world can we find ultimate fulfillment and the deepest levels of satisfaction. In this chapter we'll look at how the call to play for the kingdom in all of life includes a call to change the world.

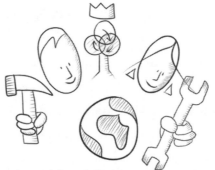

The book of Acts calls us to change the world by living lives of primary play through Christ

Beauty Will Change the World

Dostoevsky once said that "beauty will save the world." The Acts call to witness is the call to a beauty that will change the world. What is this revolutionary beauty? Missiologist J. H. Bavinck thought long and hard about how the good news of Jesus Christ spread around the world. What made it so attractive to so many people in such a wide variety of cultures? He turned to the Old Testament to find his answer. There he discovered that the key to changing the world was creating envy—to grab the heart of the world in such a way that the kings and queens of the planet would stream into Zion and join the kingdom of God (see Isaiah 60).[1] Beauty creates envy. Beauty in all its forms draws us to itself like sunlight draws a leaf. A key part of God's Eden project is to beautify a missionary people who will in turn help create the envy that brings the world home and makes it whole.

We change the world by creating envy

I can imagine some objections at this point. Envy is evil. How can we use something evil to change the world? What is surprising is how the apostle Paul describes his mission to the nations as creating envy in Romans 11:13-14: "I am talking to you Gentiles. Inasmuch as I am the apostle to the Gentiles, I take pride in my ministry in the hope that I may somehow arouse my own people to *envy* and save some of them."

Envy is simply wanting what someone else has. Envy is evil when, in taking what it wants, it hurts the other person. But here is an envy that is good. Wanting the beauty that God offers to us is a good envy. When we take that beauty, we are not hurting or depriving God but doing what he wants.

How does primary play create envy-inspiring beauty? Recall our discussion of simple and complex beauty in the Isaiah call to wow. Simple beauty is symmetrical. In the sphere of relationships, it is giving people what we owe and no more. Complex beauty, on the other hand, is not symmetrical. It is beauty that creates a harmony out of opposites. Light and dark, action and rest, life and death all combine on the canvas of a great master and produce the highest beauty known to humanity—the beauty of harmonizing opposites. If our triple delight gets complex enough, it creates this high beauty. Imagine delighting not only in success, progress and victory but also in the modern equivalents of hardships such as prison, shipwreck and slander. That's the kind of delight we see in Peter and Paul in the book of Acts. Imagine being able to delight in interactions with sworn enemies, rival ethnic groups, people across generation gaps and religious competitors in a way that produces a harmonious "whomever" that is beautiful to behold. Imagine the kind of complex delight that trusts in the "wherever" of God's new creation as we face hostile crowds, tricky tyrants, adoring friends and impossible odds. The beauty of God's love and power that is displayed by the harmony of opposites, by bringing beauty out of ashes, grabs the attention of the world's people and draws them toward the light.

The Acts call to witness is a call to display the beauty of God in three ways.

We create envy through beautiful news, beautiful community and beautiful lives. Let's look at each.

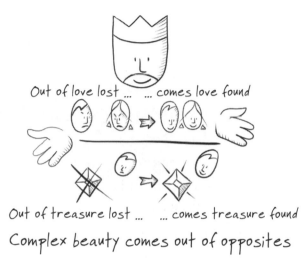

Out of love lost ... ... comes love found

Out of treasure lost ... ... comes treasure found

Complex beauty comes out of opposites

Beautiful News

Luke opens the book of Acts by mentioning that in his first book he talked about what "Jesus began to do and to teach" (Acts 1:1). This strongly implies that Acts is about what Jesus in his risen and ascended state continues to do and to teach. The book of Acts is about "ascension politics," how Jesus, the King of the World, moves the *baraka* mission of God forward, toward the finish line. It is a book about what Jesus the Davidic King continued to do and teach through his new body, his kingdom citizens on earth. This is the good news that Peter preached in Acts 2, and it has rocked the world ever since.

We must avoid the temptation to conclude that when Jesus ascended into a cloud and left the disciples' field of vision, he disappeared from geopolitical affairs and salvation history, leaving his beleaguered people to dabble in politics and to twist the arms of the rest of the world into believing. Some of the disciples would have recognized the cloud drama of Acts 1 as a reminder of the cloud drama recorded in Luke 9. Jesus took Peter, James and John up on a mountain, where a cloud moved in and transformed the whole experience. The disciples saw Jesus surrounded with radiance and saw the long-dead Moses and Elijah fully alive. In that moment Jesus was shown to be not only a man of earth but a Lord from heaven, someone who was the middle man that would bring these two planes of existence together.

The disciples would have also remembered the stories of the cloud of God's presence in the wilderness wanderings of Israel. The cloud was a sign of God's ongoing leadership of his people. Between his resurrection and ascension Christ prepared his disciples for the new politics of his kingly rule by teaching them about the kingdom of God. What was his teaching about the kingdom? Luke focuses on one important lesson that captured the essence of kingdom politics for the church in Acts.

> Then they gathered around him and asked him, "Lord, are you at this time going to restore the kingdom to Israel?"
>
> He said to them: "It is not for you to know the times or dates the Father has set by his own authority. But you will receive power when the Holy Spirit comes on you; and you will be my witnesses in Jerusalem, and in all Judea and Samaria, and to the ends of the earth." (Acts 1:6-8)

Let me highlight three important aspects of kingdom politics addressed in these verses, each of which closes a gap that had previously separated people from the mission of God.

First, there is a power gap between the King and his people. Jesus taught the disciples that the new creation has two signs: one is that Jesus will be ruling and the second is that his followers will share that rule. Jesus said to them, "Truly I tell you, at the renewal of all things, when the Son of Man sits on his glorious throne, you who have followed me will also sit on twelve thrones, judging the twelve tribes of Israel" (Matthew 19:28). Through this partnership between king and subjects, the new creation will be brought to its glorious completion; the dream of Isaiah will be realized. When the disciples ask in verse 6 whether it is time for Israel (and them!) to rule, they are not being quite as thick as they sometimes are made out to be. They are asking Jesus if Matthew 19:28 is happening before their eyes. Jesus' answer is as instructive for what it doesn't say as for what it does. He does not deny that he is ascending to the glorious throne from which he will bring about the renewal of all things. His ascension means that the first part of Matthew 19:28 is being fulfilled.

However, the second part of the verse, the rule of Israel, the people of God, is delayed until Jesus' reappearance at the end of history. Their assignment in the meantime is not to rule but to bear witness to his present rule. They are not to seek worldly power in order to demonstrate the politics of God. Rather, they are to show that the primary piece of the politics of God is already in place: Jesus is now in charge of the course of history and earthly politics. One reason why the early church of Acts seems politically indifferent is not that they are apolitical but rather that they are ultra-political: *The new emperor of all things is already in place.* They have all the political power they want or need.

A second important aspect of this political message is that the Spirit fills the gap between his total power and our almost total weakness by giving us access to his divine power. One of the primary benefits of Jesus' ascended state is that

The church in Acts was ultra-political: They believed the new emperor was already in place even though the world had not yet changed

Witness without Spirit   Witness with the Spirit
The King gives his Spirit to his church to bring effective witness and change

his citizen sons now have available the same power that Jesus had on earth, the power of the Spirit. This is the Spirit who made the world of Genesis so beautiful as he hovered over the void and brought about order.

Third, the followers of the risen and ruling Jesus fill the gap with witness. This same Spirit will flow as the body of the risen and exalted King moves through the world and bears witness to the new Eden that is coming. The Spirit will provide everything that is needed for the political witness of the church—the witness that Jesus, and not Caesar, is Lord.

Beautiful Community

Because Jesus is now King, his citizens, soon to represent every ethnic and linguistic group in the world, become part of a new community, the *ekklesia*, or called-out ones. In this new community we are no longer under the law of sin and death but under the new law of the Spirit and of life. This new community, when it is animated by the King Jesus gospel, is full of charisma and flow. This new community is filled with delight in the ever-growing diversity of the whomever it is doing life with.

This spiritual power and freedom helps defeat the injustices and ethnic hatred that has characterized human history from the beginning. In Acts 2 we see a new community of three thousand who have become followers of King Jesus and who are filled with his new power, the Spirit of God. We watch them share their lives, their money, all they own with perfect strangers who have entered the new kingdom with them. We see the new community persecuted by the world and its old politics but flourishing even as it is scattered. In chapter 6 we see it overcoming injustice when food is not being evenly shared between two very different groups of widows. In Acts 10 we see their delight in the ever-enlarging whomever when Cornelius, a Gentile, is embraced into this community. In Acts 15 we see the triumph of this delight in whomever is in his kingdom when a council of the whole church decides to eliminate all cultural

The world Christian movement is the most culturally and racially diverse movement in the world

barriers to the gospel, allowing people to enter the kingdom of Jesus through faith alone and not by becoming Jews.

When Paul talks about this charismatic community of Jesus, he delights not only in the ethnic diversity of the complex whomever but also the diversity of gifts. Those under the rule of the new King are not threatened by this diversity. He will weave the diverse backgrounds, knowledge, cultures, gifts and talents of his church into a beautiful dance that will lead the church to maturity and draw the world to its beauty (see Ephesians 4:16).

Many millennials say they love Jesus but hate the church. Yet looking around the world, we can see that Jesus is bringing his church back to life and calling young people to be a part of that resurrection project. He is using his people everywhere as change agents in his world.

One example of the renewal of the church around the world is Mavuno Church in Nairobi, Kenya. Started in 2005 with a handful of people, it has grown to over five thousand in all of its campuses. Some of those campuses are in places such as Berlin, Germany, and Kampala, Uganda. The main campus of the church used to be at Bellevue Cinema, an old drive-in theater transformed for Mavuno's purposes. Their target audience is emerging adults who are tired of churches where they feel judged. They welcome those on the margins of the church and invite them to join them on an adventure turning "ordinary people into fearless influencers in society." The church does this through the "Mavuno Marathon." The marathon begins when university-trained and upwardly mobile "Mike and Makena" (Mavuno's handles for their target audience) attend a Sunday morning or Saturday night service. The music is contemporary, the topics are relevant and the delivery is closer to a high-level television talk show than a conventional worship service. Yet the message is clearly one of biblical truth and the relevance of the gospel for all of life.

As "Mike and Makena" (M and M in Makuno shorthand) grow in their interest they are encouraged to take a Mizizi class. Mizizi is Swahili for "roots." The Mizizi book is colorful and fun but covers key lessons on what it means to be a Christian, including practical issues such as sexuality, money management and relationships. Upon completion of the class, M and M are encouraged to commit

Mavuno Church: "Turning ordinary people into fearless influencers of society"

to a weekly life group to study the Bible. About 80 percent of Mavuno's regular attenders belong to a life group. But the journey does not end there. From the life group M and M attend further training that focuses on renewing several key areas of national life (family and friends, economics and business, governance and justice, entertainment and media, etc.). Through this training Mavuno members are able to discover their "frontline ministry" in one or more of these key areas. A significant frontline ministry at Mavuno is prison ministry. Every week Mavuno members seeks to serve the spiritual and material needs of thousands of incarcerated Kenyans. Their level of involvement and impact on the prison system is nothing short of remarkable. Once M and M have identified their frontline ministry they are well on their way to being "fearless influencers of society."[2]

Beautiful Lives

The call to witness in the book of Acts is not just a call to church involvement or to become a pastor or missionary. The call to witness is also a call to be salt and light wherever you are. It is a call that takes an African politician, turns him into a citizen of the new kingdom of God and sends him back to his queen and continent with a new message and lifestyle (Acts 8).

The call to witness in the book of Acts is about everyday people like Tabitha and Lydia. Tabitha is known for her good works and is raised from the dead by

Tabitha and witness of service and miracles

Lydia and witness of business and hospitality

Barnabas and witness of encouragement and friendship

The call to witness is a call to be salt and light missionaries wherever you are

Peter. She does not become a crosscultural missionary but carries on her good works. Lydia is a businesswoman who lives in Europe. She becomes a follower of the new King and uses her gift of hospitality to help change her world. Long before Barnabas went into full-time ministry, he used his gift of friendship and encouragement to mobilize others, including Paul, to service in the kingdom. The beauty of everyday Christians being filled with the fullness of the Spirit as they dance with God and go about their everyday life in offices, schools, stadiums and homes is a huge part of creating kingdom envy and changing one's world.[3]

At Play in the Fields of the Lord: New Witnesses

This kind of beautiful witness is not just in the book of Acts; it is going on around the world. It is there in the new churches of the Global South that are lifting people out of poverty and oppression and showing the liberating power of the great king. But it is not just in the Global South. Beautiful witness is rising even in our secular cities closer to home. Founded in the heart of New York City in 1989 by Tim Keller and his wife, Kathy, Redeemer Presbyterian Church has grown to twenty-five hundred attenders with an average age in their early thirties. The church has helped start over two hundred other churches around the world. Tim Keller is widely known for applying the gospel creatively and powerfully to all of life. He writes deep and searching books on apologetics and Christian living that have made the *New York Times* Best Seller list. But the real story of Redeemer Church is not the numbers or the notoriety. It is all about recovering the beauty of the message and living it out in beautiful lives. They have groups that focus on bringing Christian beauty to the arts, to political issues and to the renewal of work, or what the church calls "vocational discipleship." The Center for Faith and Work was started in 2002 in order to advance this vision of faith, work and life integration. Keller has summarized ten "shifts" they are making from traditional forms of Christianity into ones that shine with more biblical beauty, seeking to create missional envy in the watching world.[4]

How do we change the world? By creating envy, a good envy that draws the world toward God's *baraka* project and toward its Lord. And how do we create this beautiful envy? By being fully alive followers of Jesus that flow out of a life

Change from	Change to
1. individual salvation	1. Gospel changes everything
2. Being good	2. Being saved
3. Cheap grace	3. Costly grace (aware of sin)
4. Heaven is "up there"	4. Christ will come again to this earth
5. God is value-add to us	5. God enables us to contribute to his work on earth
6. Idols of this world	6. Living for God
7. Disdain of this world	7. Engaged in this world
8. "Bowling Alone"	8. Accepting community
9. People matter	9. Institutions matter
10. Christian superiority	10. God can work through anyone (common grace)

The Message of Redeemer Church

of triple delight. We must go deeper into the complex flow of the dance of God and delight in whatever his Spirit gives us to do, in whomever the Spirit asks us to do life with and for, and in the mighty Father whose kingdom of love not only watches over us with total care but whose mighty arm guides the world toward the new creation and the renewal of all things.

To achieve this powerful work-life balance, to enter into the mission of God, requires hearing and balancing a cluster of God's calls. We must believe in this mission like Abraham. We must work for this mission like Adam and Eve in Eden. We must be liberated for this mission like the Israelites in the exodus. We must fight for delight in the people of mission like David. We must wow with Isaiah about the mission's stunning climax and love with all the passion of the singers to show that the mission restores all of life. When we dance like Jesus and witness like Acts we become playful partners in the new creation, and the world begins to change.

Let's go back to our dream. You look again at the gleaming city on the plain that rose from fire and ashes. You wake up from your dream and look out your window at the world around you. It is a world you know well: the mall, school, office, stadium, gym, the wrong side of the tracks, the homes of friends and neighbors, the church on the corner, the town hall, the cinema. Time, folly and death can turn the skyline of your personal world into ashes and anguish. Lady Wisdom, however, can turn it into beauty. Becoming part of the people of God around the world, those who belong to the mission of God, will make the difference between folly's blight and wisdom's beauty.

Our world needs wisdom workers, kingdom players who use the power of delight in all they do to change the world. I invite you to join the dance of delight. As you play your way through the joys and tears of modern life, through the cities in ruins and the wreckage of modernity, green shoots will spring up everywhere. Trees of life, of playful work, prayerful play and deep love, will grow in Brooklyn and Buenos Aires and in the back of beyond. Out of ashes, beauty. Out of mourning, dancing. Out of folly, a world and a humanity fully and forever alive.

Thinking It Through

1. Jot down your reaction to the idea that beauty can change the world. Have you seen examples in your own life where you made a significant choice or change on the basis of beautiful envy?

2. This chapter argues that the good news is both political and private. In what sense is it political? How does it differ from conventional politics?

3. The beautiful news that Jesus is the dominant although unseen force in local and global politics calls on those who play for the kingdom to relativize the importance of local politics and the negative claims of each side about the other. In light of the good news of Jesus, what could be said to members of the political right or left about making absolute condemnations or promises based on human politics and power?

4. Why don't millennials like the church? What are the benefits of beautiful communities of Christ, such as the new church of Jerusalem in Acts 2, that emerging adults need to know about?

5. What features of the Mavuno Church stand out to you? In what ways do they help people achieve the kind of rich work-life balance that we have talked about in this book? What impresses you about Redeemer Church's witness and its ten shifts?

6. What would "beautiful play" look like at home, at school, at the office or at church? How might the triple delight of beautiful play create life-changing envy in those places? How can you cultivate this habit of thinking and living in your particular job and life?

7. The mission of Christians must be based on the mission of God. Since God's Eden project is happening all around us, we are called to join him in a balanced way in the four areas of changing hearts, perfecting churches, restoring the environment and building nations. Which of the four areas are you most concerned about at present? Which areas of his mission do you need to develop in your life? How can you become more involved in these areas of mission?

8. Where are you in your life journey? Which path (wisdom or folly) are you on? What action do you need to take to become a wisdom worker and become fully alive?

Taking Action

1. Consider starting a book club on changing the world. Read books that would be relevant to the mission of God and your calling in that great mission. A

useful resource for missional thinking about political and economic systems can be found in Bob Goudzwaard, Mark Vander Vennen and David Van Heemst's book *Hope in Troubled Times: A New Vision for Confronting Global Crises* (Grand Rapids: Baker Academic, 2007). Jonathan Haidt offers a balanced look at why we need both conservative and liberal voices in our nations and churches in *The Righteous Mind: Why Good People Are Divided by Politics and Religion* (New York: Pantheon, 2012). A more theologically oriented study is Chris Wright, *The Mission of God's People* (Grand Rapids: Zondervan, 2010). For the more ambitious, Chris Wright's *The Mission of God: Unlocking the Bible's Grand Narrative* (Downers Grove, IL: IVP Academic, 2006) is an excellent exploration of this central theme in the Scriptures.

2. Read through the Bible missionally. A few years ago I read through the Bible asking just three questions of each chapter: What does the passage say about the mission of God? What does it say about the God of mission? What does it say about my role in his mission? The Bible came alive for me in a way that I had never experienced before. Consider taking a year or two to read through the Bible asking these questions. What might be some benefits for your career and calling?

3. James Choung's "Big Story" is an excellent tool for explaining to friends the good news of the mission of God. It can be found online at www.jameschoung .net. Take a look at his approach. What are the strengths and weaknesses of this presentation of the gospel? Who do you need to share this story with?

Notes

Introduction

[1]Dan Roam, *Blah, Blah, Blah: What to Do When Words Don't Work* (New York: Portfolio Hardcover, 2011).

[2]See www.theparisreview.org/interviews/2977/the-art-of-fiction-no-81-milan-kundera.

[3]Ibid., emphasis added.

[4]Colossians 1:16-17 indirectly references Proverbs 8 when it says "For in him all things were created: things in heaven and on earth, visible and invisible, whether thrones or powers or rulers or authorities; all things have been created through him and for him. He is before all things, and in him all things hold together." Colossians 2:3 seems to distinguish between wisdom's personification in Proverbs 8 and wisdom's perfect embodiment in Jesus: "in whom are hidden all the treasures of wisdom and knowledge."

Chapter 1: Lady Wisdom's Call to Play

[1]Abby Ellin, "Work-Life Balance Off Kilter, Research Finds," ABC News, April 19, 2013, http://abcnews.go.com/business/t/blogEntry?id=18996329&ref=https%3A%2F%2Fwww.google.com%2F. Accessed October 30, 2013.

[2]See Bird's articles and blog at worklifebalance.com.

[3]Tremper Longman III, *Proverbs* (Grand Rapids: Baker, 2006), Kindle ed., location 4171.

[4]Samuel Terrien, *Till the Heart Sings: A Biblical Theology of Manhood and Womenhood* (Grand Rapids: Eerdmans, 2004), p. 87.

[5]Longman, *Proverbs*, location 4159.

[6]Hugh Matlack, "The Play of Wisdom," *Currents in Theology and Mission* 15 (1988): 426.

Chapter 2: Play and Flow

[1]Stuart Brown, *Play: How It Shapes the Brain, Opens the Imagination, and Invigorates the Soul* (New York: Penguin, 2009), p. 5.

[2]Ibid., p. 6.

[3]Ibid., p. 7.

[4]Jane McGonagall, *Reality Is Broken: Why Games Make Us Better and How They Can Change the World* (London: Penguin, 2011), Kindle ed., location 159.

[5]Ibid., location 168.

[6]Ibid., location 375.

[7]Mihaly Csikszentmihalyi, *Flow: The Psychology of Optimal Experience* (San Francisco: Harper-Collins, 2008), Kindle ed.

[8]Ibid., location 220.

[9]McGonagall, *Reality Is Broken,* location 585.

[10]Ibid., location 440.

[11]Csikszentmihalyi, *Flow,* location 391.

[12]Ibid., location 282.

Chapter 3: The Eden Call to Work

[1]Jordan Weismann, "53% of Recent College Grads Are Jobless or Underemployed—How?" *The Atlantic,* April 23, 2012, www.theatlantic.com/business/archive/2012/04/53-of-recent-college-grads-are-jobless-or-underemployed-how/256237.

[2]Max Weber, *The Protestant Ethic and the Spirit of Capitalism* (Mineola, NY: Dover Publications, 2003).

[3]R. Paul Stevens, *The Other Six Days: Vocation, Work and Ministry in Biblical Perspective* (Grand Rapids: Eerdmans, 1999), p. 107.

[4]Tim Keller, *Every Good Endeavor: Connecting Your Work to God's Work* (New York: Dutton, 2012), p. 34.

[5]Ibid., p. 58.

[6]For a fuller discussion of the impact of Aristotle's views on work in the West, see Tim Keller, *Every Good Endeavor* (New York: Dutton, 2012), pp. 45-46.

[7]Ibid., p. 59.

[8]Ibid., p. 15.

[9]Ibid.

[10]Ibid., p. 16.

Chapter 5: The Abraham Call to Believe

[1]Cf. Christian Smith with Melinda Lundquist Denton, *Soul Searching: The Religious and Spiritual Lives of American Teenagers* (New York: Oxford University Press, 2005), and Christian Smith, Kari Christoffersen, Hilary Davidson and Patricia Snell Herzog, *Lost in Transition: The Dark Side of Emerging Adulthood* (New York: Oxford University Press, 2011).

[2]Smith, *Soul Searching,* Kindle ed., location 3394.

[3]Ibid., location 3403.

[4]Christopher Wright, *The Mission of God: Unlocking the Bible's Grand Narrative* (Downers Grove, IL: InterVarsity Press, 2006), Kindle ed., location 2622.

Chapter 6: The Exodus Call to Freedom

[1]Originally part of a Harvard Class Day Address in 1988. Wolfe later discussed his views on America's fifth freedom in Dorothy Scura, ed., *Conversations with Tom Wolfe* (Jackson: University of Mississippi Press, 1990), pp. 250-51.

[2]Os Guinness, *A Free People's Suicide: Sustainable Freedom and America's Future* (Downers Grove, IL: InterVarsity Press, 2012).

[3]Martin Luther, *The Small Catechism* (St. Louis, MO: Concordia, 1986).

[4]Abraham Heschel, *The Sabbath* (1951; reprint, New York: Farrar Straus & Giroux, 2005).

[5]Eugene Peterson, *Working the Angles: The Shape of Pastoral Integrity* (Grand Rapids: Eerdmans, 1993), p. 71.

Chapter 7: The David Call to Relationships

[1]Stephen Covey and Jennifer Colosimo, *Great Work, Great Career: How to Create Your Ultimate Job and Make an Extraordinary Contribution* (Salt Lake City: Franklin Covey, 2009), Kindle ed., locations 1357, 1364, 1372.

[2]"Together in Poverty, Apart in Riches," *Daily Nation* (Nairobi, Kenya), September, 24, 2011, p. 17.

[3]Tremper Longman III and Dan Allender, *Cry of the Soul: How Our Emotions Reveal Our Deepest Questions About God* (Colorado Springs: NavPress, 1994).

Chapter 8: The Singers' Call to Lovemaking

[1]See C. S. Lewis, *The Four Loves* (New York: Harcourt Brace Jovanovich, 1991).

[2]Tremper Longman III, *The Song of Songs,* New International Commentary on the Old Testament (Grand Rapids: Eerdmans, 2001), pp. 2-3.

[3]Cf. Timothy Keller with Kathy Keller, *The Meaning of Marriage: Facing the Complexities of Commitment with the Wisdom of God* (New York: Dutton, 2011), p. 185.

Chapter 9: The Isaiah Call to Wow

[1]Jonathan Haidt, *The Happiness Hypothesis: Finding Modern Truth in Ancient Wisdom* (New York: Basic Books, 2006).

[2]Anne Lamott, *Help, Thanks, Wow: The Three Essential Prayers* (New York: Riverhead, 2012), p. 70.

[3]For a study of Edwards on beauty, see Owen Strachan and Douglas Sweeney, eds., *Jonathan*

Edwards on Beauty (Chicago: Moody Press, 2010). Edwards's most important works on beauty are his two dissertations, *On the End for Which God Created the World* and *The Nature of True Virtue*. These two works are found in volume 8 of the Yale edition of his collected works. They can be accessed online at edwards.yale.edu.

[4]See the discussion on the ascension of Christ and his current rule in N. T. Wright, *Surprised by Hope: Rethinking Heaven, the Resurrection and the Mission of the Church* (San Francisco: Harper Collins, 2007), chap. 7.

Chapter 10: The Jesus Call to Dance

[1]Timothy Keller, *Jesus the King: Understanding the Life and Death of the Son of God* (New York: Riverhead, 2013), p. 3.

[2]C. S. Lewis, *Mere Christianity* (New York: Macmillan, 1977), p. 151, quoted in Keller, *Jesus the King*, p. 4.

[3]Keller, *Jesus the King*, p. 5.

[4]Christopher Wright, *The Mission of God: Unlocking the Bible's Grand Narrative* (Downers Grove, IL: InterVarsity Press, 2006), Kindle ed., location 4262.

Chapter 11: The Acts Call to Change the World

[1]J. H. Bavinck, *Introduction to the Science of Missions* (Philadelphia: Presbyterian and Reformed Publishing, 1960), p. 47.

[2]For more information about Mavuno Church, see their website at mavuno.org.

[3]Tabitha's story is found in Acts 9, Lydia's in Acts 16 and Barnabas's in Acts 9.

[4]Tim Keller, *Every Good Endeavor: Connecting Your Work to God's Work* (New York: Dutton, 2012), Kindle ed., location 2992.